D1317568

A Field Guide to

CANADIAN

SCOTT McCALLUM & VICTORIA WALSH

Photography by JUAN LUNA
Prop styling by VIRGINIE MARTOCQ
Food and drink styling by VICTORIA WALSH

COCKTAILS

appetite
by RANDOM HOUSE

Copyright © 2015 Scott McCallum and Victoria Walsh
Photography copyright © 2015 Juan Luna

All rights reserved. The use of any part of this publication, reproduced, transmitted in any form or
by any means electronic, mechanical, photocopying, recording or otherwise, or stored in a retrieval
system without the prior written consent of the publisher—or in the case of photocopying or other
reprographic copying, license from the Canadian Copyright Licensing Agency—is an infringement
of the copyright law.

Appetite by Random House® is a registered trademark of Random House LLC.

Library and Archives Canada Cataloguing in Publication is available upon request.

Print ISBN: 978-0-449-01663-3
e-book ISBN: 978-0-449-01664-0

Cover and book design by CS Richardson
Prop styling by Virginie Martocq
Food and drink styling by Victoria Walsh

Printed and bound in China

Published in Canada by Appetite by Random House®,
a division of Random House of Canada Limited,
a Penguin Random House Company

www.penguinrandomhouse.ca

10 9 8 7 6 5 4 3 2 1

appetite
by RANDOM HOUSE

Penguin
Random
House

To Margaret, who has always been there.

To Cathy and Don, for their constant love and support.

To those who inspired, helped and encouraged us to take this journey.

And to this great land.

CONTENTS

Introduction ix
Tricks & Tools 1

COAST TO COAST TO COAST
The Canadian 14
Hot Toddy 17
The Great White Caesar 18
East–Meets–West Coast Caesar 19
Gin & Tonic 22
Kir & Kir Royale 24
Sour Slush 28
The Double Double 31

THE WEST
Jack with One Eye 41
Sea Island Iced Tea 42
Saskatoon Julep 43
Canadian Winter's Punch 44
The Oenophile 46
Rocket Richardonnay 47
Ogopogo Sour 49
El Camino 2.0 50
Bob & Doug's Strange Brew 52
Sunken Port 53
What's Up, Doc? 54
The Emperor 56
Smoky Lake Old-Fashioned 58
Campfire Flip 59
Butchart Garden Swizzle 61

THE PRAIRIES
Whoop-Up Bug Juice 68
A Bit of Northern Hospitality 70

Chinook Sangria 71
The Pearl Punch 73
Spiced Peach Spritz 74
Bonita Applebaum 76
Gins & Needles 77
The Stampeder 78
The Loose Jaw 81
The Flatlander's Fizz 82
Devil's Barrel 83
Saskatoon Berry & Wheat Beer
   Cocktail 84
Prairie Caesar 86
Lord Stanley's Punch 87
Flintabbatey Flonatin's Sunless
   City Sipper 89
Golden Boy 90

THE MIDDLE
Pimm's Spin 99
Balsam Blend 101
Man about Chinatown 102
PTB 103
Spadina Splash 104
The Torontonian 106
Ronald Clayton 107
The Gardiner 108
Peary Punch 110
North of 44 111
Celery Rickey 113
The Canadian R&R 114
Prince Edward Bounty 117
Canadian Rye Dirty Martini 118
The Alchemist 119

Caribou 120

The Polar Vortex 121

Saison Royale 122

The Boreal Cotton-Candy
   Cocktail 125

Sweet Fern G&T 126

Saucier's Seigniory Special 127

Black Beaux-Arts Fizz 128

La Pomme du Diable 130

THE EAST

Fiddlehead Martini 139

The Loyalist 140

The Coupe de Cartier 141

Acadian Driftwood 142

Magnetic Hill Sour 144

The Bright Red 145

Sparkling Watermelon Sipper 147

The Nellie J. Banks 148

Wild Rose Negroni 150

The Post Sunset 151

Lavender-Blueberry Sparkler 152

Winter Garden 155

Pumpkin Colada 156

1749 Negroni 158

The Corroded Nail 159

Hot Buttered Rum 160

Cold Buttered Rum 162

Labrador Iced Tea 163

St. John's Sling 164

The 52% 166

Nan's Kitchen 167

THE NORTH

Yukon Gold Rush 173

Arctic Martinez 175

The Bush Pilot 176

The Spell of the Yukon 177

The Yukon Sourtoe Shot 178

THE BASICS

Syrup 101 182
   Simple Syrup 182
   Simple Syrup Variations 182

Infusion 101 184
   Infusions 184

Tonic 186

Canadian Cocktail Cherries 188

Blackberry Grenadine 189

Traditional-Style Grenadine 189

Raspberry Cordial 190

Black Walnut Orgeat 192

Tomato-Clam Juice 193

FOOD & COCKTAILS

Oyster Guide 194

Canadian Cheese 196

A Drinkable Garden 198

TO BE CONTINUED . . .

*Inspirations, Resources
   & Recommended Reading* 202

Conversion Chart 203

Acknowledgements 204

Index 206

INTRODUCTION

Welcome to *Canadian Cocktails*, our boozy celebration of True North spirit. For this book, we aimed to capture and create some of the most sensational sips, from sea to shining sea. We scoured the country to find the best ingredients; to consult the most accomplished bartenders, distillers and other makers; and to get to know the land, people and history that inform the flavours and character that the cocktails embody.

In these pages, you'll find tips and tricks for the home host, smart techniques from Canada's top bartenders, suggestions for how to stock the ultimate Canadian bar, and even a sprinkle of travel advice, with highlights from our coast-to-coast cocktail conquest.

But first, some background. A few years ago, we got engaged next to a sunny container garden on our apartment rooftop in Toronto, which Scott built secretly, using his long-dormant green thumb. This small urban garden was a gift, a marker for the beginning of our lives together and the catalyst for a new urban homestead-style life for both of us. Thanks to Scott's newly unearthed farming roots, our garden flourished, yielding a bounty of fruits and vegetables (which you'll see were put to use in the book's recipes). This, coupled with Victoria's career as food writer and stylist, kept our lives revolving around food and drink—local and, whenever possible, homegrown. It was only natural that our try-anything-and-use-everything approach to cooking would broaden into a passion for making garden-fresh cocktails too. (Of course, being talented tipplers helped our cause as well.) We started with basic homemade drinks like hot pepper–infused Caesars, and then began playing with herbal simple syrups, infusions, tinctures, bitters and liqueurs. Eventually, we moved beyond our garden to Canada's garden, on the hunt for exciting, largely unexplored and distinctly Canadian flavours.

While we were learning, experimenting and searching for the best Canadian cocktails, it became apparent that there is a lack of comprehensive work on the subject. Don't get us wrong, we love a good Caesar, but it is not the only cocktail to be fashioned in this country. We decided it was time to solidify Canada's place in the international cocktail canon. That's how we came to the idea for *Canadian Cocktails*, a book dedicated to perfectly crafted, Canadian-infused and -inspired drinks. And so we kept our ears to the ground and noses to the coupes while partaking in a lot of recipe alchemy, spirit tasting and treasure hunting across the country.

After years of exploration and discovery, we are excited to finally share our findings and recipes. This isn't a definitive guide, but rather a medium for showcasing the bartenders and producers who make the cocktail scene in Canada so strong and impressive. This book is a jumping-off point. Our hope is to get your creative juices flowing, and to use this book's guidelines as inspiration for your own experiments, whether it's stirring up classic drinks at home or seeking out delicious libations while travelling.

This field guide starts with the basics. In the next chapter you'll find tips on what you'll need to craft a stellar cocktail—technique, glassware, equipment and, of course, great liquor. Next you'll find tales of our Canadian cocktail pursuit, some nods to the history that shaped our drinking landscape and shout-outs to some of our favourite places in the country, all accompanied by refreshing and purely Canadian drink recipes, many of which are our own creative concoctions, others shared by a fantastic selection of Canada's most passionate bartenders.

In proper celebratory fashion, we show our dedication to this great country in the form of a drink. Cheers to Canada!

TRICKS & TOOLS

*Here's our primer on how to make excellent drinks every time,
and the tools you'll need to prepare them.*

BASIC COCKTAIL TECHNIQUES

PREPARE AND STORE ICE This simple ingredient is often overlooked and taken for granted—ice can taste funny or be the wrong shape (causing it to melt too quickly or not dilute the drink enough) or, the worst faux pas of all, not having enough on hand. But these mistakes are easily avoidable. Use filtered water, when available, to make ice. Invest in multiple standard ice cube trays plus a **king cube mould**, to make large ice cubes. When preparing for a party, set several trays and moulds on a baking sheet, fill with water and freeze. Place freshly prepared ice in large resealable freezer bags. This prevents freezer odours from absorbing while allowing you to stockpile. When it comes to crushed ice, cheat and buy store-bought or crush your own by pounding regular cubes in a resealable plastic bag. Just cover a partially sealed bag with a kitchen towel and use a rubber mallet.

CHILL A GLASS An essential step in helping to maintain optimal cocktail temperature is chilling a glass. Often, simply tucking a glass in the freezer works well, but when left too long, delicate glassware can crack. Keep your eye on it or set a timer for a few minutes. Alternately, fill a glass with ice and cold water and let it stand while you prepare your cocktail. When ready, discard ice and water, shaking off any excess water. Add fresh ice, if using in the cocktail.

MEASURE Cocktails are like baking: when it comes to measuring, precision is essential. Be sure to use appropriate tools, such as dry measuring cups for dry ingredients (we use the scoop-and-swipe method) and **measuring spoons**, liquid measuring cups and **jiggers** for liquids.

There are many types of bitters bottles and dashers available, and it can be difficult to be exact. Add a dash by inverting a dasher with a quick flick of your wrist. When using a **dropper**, draw and use what can be released with one squeeze. You may even want to use slightly less than what is drawn when squeezing into your drink. For dashes and drops, err on the side of caution; it doesn't take much to overpower a drink. Taste and adjust to your preference.

For cocktail recipes calling for egg white, our preference is to use small eggs. If you only have large ones, lightly beat the egg white in a small bowl, then measure out ¾ oz.

STIR AND SHAKE Both shaking and stirring work to chill and incorporate cocktail ingredients. Shaking adds more air bubbles, creating a vibrant and airy drink. Stirring delicately combines elements, preserving the spirit's true character. Citrus, dairy, cream (including cream liqueur) and egg drinks are shaken. Spirit-forward cocktails are simply stirred.

For the shaking method, a **Boston shaker**, a combo of **cocktail shaker base** and **mixing glass** top, is commonly used. We also suggest both a stainless-steel cocktail shaker base and a stainless-steel top (slightly smaller so it fits into the base). This combo chills a drink swiftly while allowing you to sense the temperature change. To prepare, add ingredients to the base. Fill with ice cubes. Insert top and smack downward to seal. The metal will contract and form an even tighter seal during shaking. Hold both ends securely while maintaining pressure. Shake back and forth, holding the shaker above your shoulders, parallel to the ground, for approximately 12 to 15 seconds. Times vary depending on ice size or certain recipe requirements. We tend to stop when our fingertips experience a touch of brain freeze. Open by twisting the top, or break the seal by pinching the shaker base and hitting the outside of the base

with the heel of your hand. This should help release the seal.

For stirring, you can use a basic **mixing glass** or a **Japanese-style mixing glass**, which is beautiful but comes with a higher price tag. You can also use a cocktail shaker base, as it's wide enough to properly stir and you can feel the temperature of the drink change. When our recipes call for a mixing glass, use any of these options. Add ingredients, then fill three-quarters full with ice cubes. Place the backside of a **barspoon** against the mixing glass in between the ice and the glass. Gently hold the spoon handle between your index finger and thumb. Use your middle finger to push at the point closest to you and your index finger to pull when it is furthest away. Repeat this process and it will soon become seamless. The stirring shouldn't make a lot of noise; sloshing and splashing indicate that you are creating unwanted air bubbles. Care is more important than speed.

STRAIN Strain shaken drinks using a **Hawthorne strainer** and stirred ones using a **julep strainer.** Some recipes require a double strain, which is done by also pouring the liquid through a **fine-mesh strainer.** This removes particles and small ice chips from your cocktail. We prefer this method for delicately flavoured drinks, for those served over a single large ice cube and especially for those served neat (without ice).

For a cocktail served over crushed ice, it's not necessary to double strain, but we like to in order to remove any bits or ice chips, which could further dilute the drink.

DRY SHAKE For a cocktail calling for an egg, whether whole or just the white, a dry shake is required. "Dry shake" refers to pre-shaking the ingredients together without ice. This method "cooks" the eggs while helping to create the desired frothy consistency. A proper dry shake takes about 1 minute. Pressure within the shaker builds the more you shake, so hold on tight. For drinks that call for both egg and cream, wait and add the cream along with the ice, otherwise it may curdle. When using eggs, we strongly recommend using local, farm-fresh. Many traditional and modern cocktail drinks call for the use of raw egg or egg white (you'll find several throughout these pages). Please note the consumption of raw egg is not suggested for pregnant, elderly or immuno-compromised persons.

MUDDLE Muddling adds serious flavour to your cocktails. Add the muddled ingredient to the cocktail shaker or mixing glass. Top with a small amount of syrup or alcohol. Using a **muddler**, mash with a slight twisting motion. Be gentle with fresh herbs to avoid bruising or bringing out bitter flavours. Some ingredients, like fresh fruit or vegetables, may need more vigorous muddling in order to release the juices, sugars and oils. We suggest fine straining muddled drinks when they are prepared in a cocktail shaker, as opposed to pouring directly into the glass.

STERILIZE AND USE JARS Wash the **jar, lid and ring** with very hot soapy water or run them through a cycle in the dishwasher just before using. For the best seal, use new lids each time. It's fine to reuse the rings. Always leave at least ½ inch (1 cm) of headspace. Before sealing, wipe the jar rims clean with a damp cloth. Label and date before storing.

FLOAT To float an alcohol, rest the back of a barspoon over the surface of the drink without submerging it. Pour the ingredient slowly over the spoon so that it floats across the surface of the drink.

RINSE For a recipe calling for a rinsed glass, pour a very small amount of the ingredient into the glass. Swirl to coat. Shake off any excess. A shortcut is to spritz the glass with the ingredient using an atomizer.

STORE BUBBLY Store your bottle of leftover bubbly with the handle of a small **silver spoon** dangling into the mouth of the bottle. We are fuzzy on the science but we find it helps maintain the fizz for a day or two.

PREP CITRUS Always remove stickers from citrus and thoroughly wash the fruit. Dry with a kitchen towel. We strongly recommend using only freshly squeezed citrus juice: store-bought carries a completely different flavour and has not been tested in any of the recipes in this book. When preparing, first roll the fruit under your palm for ease when juicing. Ensure accuracy by pouring through a fine-mesh strainer to remove pulp and seeds before measuring. Use a **rasp** to grate citrus peel.

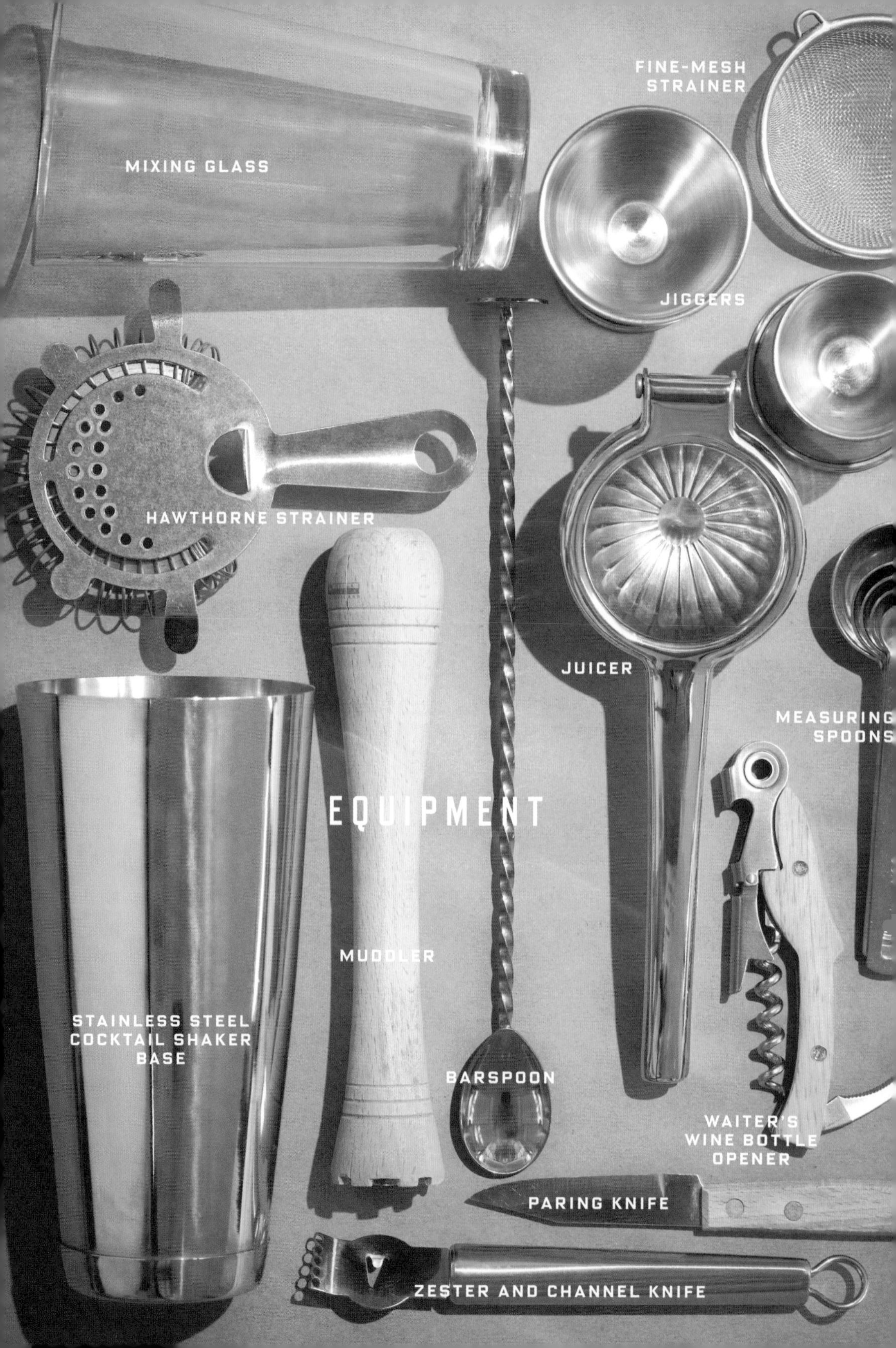

MIXING GLASS

FINE-MESH
STRAINER

JIGGERS

HAWTHORNE STRAINER

JUICER

MEASURING
SPOONS

EQUIPMENT

STAINLESS STEEL
COCKTAIL SHAKER
BASE

MUDDLER

BARSPOON

WAITER'S
WINE BOTTLE
OPENER

PARING KNIFE

ZESTER AND CHANNEL KNIFE

SWISS PEELER

CUTTING BOARD

JAR, LID
AND RING

FUNNEL

STRAW

SILVER
SPOON

COCKTAIL
SKEWER

KING ICE CUBE MOLD

EYEDROPPER
AND BOTTLE

DECORATIVE
SWIZZLE STICK

JULEP
STRAINER

JAPANESE MIXING GLASS

SMALL LADLE

CHEESECLOTH

ABSINTHE
SPOON

WOODEN SPOON

RASP

SWIZZLE STICK

GARNISH GUIDE

CITRUS TWISTS, WISPS AND STRIPS Use a channel knife to pull very thin twists of peel. Use a **Swiss peeler** to pull a small disc-shaped wisp of peel. To prepare larger strips of peel, use a Swiss peeler to pull a long strip from the citrus as you hold it over the glass, releasing some of the oils into the cocktail. With either small wisps or strips, gently pinch, peel side out, misting oils over surface of the drink. Rub the peel around the outside rim of the glass, adding more citrus aroma and flavour to the cocktail. For wisps, cut a thin slit in the centre so that it can fit snugly onto the rim of a glass. Add, garnish or discard depending on the drink.

FLAME Add complex caramel and slight burnt aromas by flaming citrus oils over the drink. Carefully light a match and hold 2 inches over the drink. Hold a large citrus strip, peel side out, between the thumb and forefinger of your other hand, 1 inch or so away from the drink. Squeeze to express the oils, sending them through the flame and down into the drink. Don't hold citrus too close to the flame or you may overpower the drink with a bitter, charred flavour. Also be careful not to light or hold the match too close to the drink or sulphur aromas will be transferred to it.

HERBS Fresh herbs add complex aromas to cocktails. Release their essential oils by clapping between the palms of your hands. Lightly wipe the outside rim of the glass with the herbs, transferring their fragrant oils and flavour before adding them to the drink.

RIMMER Place the rimmer on a small plate. Slice a small wedge from citrus, cut a shallow slit into the flesh, then pinch around the rim of the cocktail glass to moisten. Turn the outside rim of the glass in the rimmer.

CHERRIES AND OLIVES Cherries and olives are two garnishes best served using a **cocktail skewer** so that they can be easily fished out from the drink then enjoyed.

NATURAL GARNISHES AND RECIPES Within these recipes we call for some ingredients that may be wild and foraged, such as pine needles and rose petals. When foraging, always be completely confident in your identification and avoid areas with pesticides or pollution. Also, thoroughly wash everything.

STEP-BY-STEP GARNISHING
WISPS

Step 1: Pull a wisp of peel

Step 2: Pinch to mist oils

Step 3: Rub exterior rim

Step 4: Cut slit

Step 5: Fasten wisp

Step 6: Serve

Step 1: Pull long strip

Step 1: Snip

Step 2: Pinch with peel side out

Step 2: Clap then rub rim

Step 3: Rub rim, add and serve

Step 3: Serve

THE BASIC BAR

AROMATIC BITTERS This essential cocktail ingredient is non-potable (meaning it's not relished straight). It's a makeup of tinctures rounded out with bittering elements. Bitters are used to adjust and modify drinks to your liking. They lend dryness, to help balance sweetness while adding flavour. Stock a bottle of versatile aromatic bitters; classic Angostura bitters are widely available and can usually be found in the grocery aisle. More fantastic classic-style aromatic options include Boker's and Bittered Sling Kensington Dry Aromatic. If you want to expand your collection, there are a lot of options on the market to choose from—start with orange and Peychaud's, or cherry. Collecting bitters can become addictive, as they have a long bar shelf life.

GIN Gin is a neutral-based spirit distilled and macerated with a variety of botanicals: citrus peel, coriander and others, but primarily juniper. Having one classic London dry gin, such as Beefeater, is a must for recreating traditional cocktails. There are several subcategories of gin; all are worth exploring. When you're ready to expand, look for Old Tom (subtle flavour and slightly sweeter), genever (malt wine–based), cask (aged) and contemporary gins (usually with less juniper, emphasizing other flavours).

ORANGE LIQUEUR Have a citrus-spiked liqueur on hand, as it's often called upon in cocktail recipes. Brands vary in intensity and sometimes viscosity; have at least one, such as Triple Sec, Grand Marnier, Cointreau or, our favourite, Dry Curacao (less sweet than the others).

RUM Distilled from sugar cane or sugar cane by-product, most commonly molasses, rum has diverse production methods and styles, including white, gold/amber, spiced and dark. Each is worthy of earning a spot in your bar. Flavour profiles range from vanilla, cloves or cinnamon and even to mango, coconut, coffee or pumpkin. Some other choice additions to an estimable collection are rhum agricole, overproof, vintage, navy and premium aged rum.

VERMOUTH Stock your bar with both sweet (or "Italian," which is available in red or white versions) and dry (also sometimes called "French"). Quality options are reasonably priced and worth the extra investment. Our favourites include Dolin de Chambéry (both sweet and dry) and Carpano Antica Formula (sweet). As with most fortified wines, the alcohol percentage of vermouth is low—approximately 15 to 19%—so it perishes quickly when left on the counter. Store tightly capped in the fridge for up to 3 months.

VODKA While it's usually potato-derived, vodka is also sometimes made from other vegetables or fruits. The presence of vodka on an essentials list is debatable. It's not that we dislike this neutral spirit, but we would be remiss to not point out that it typically boasts more alcohol content than flavour profile. That said, some of the great Canadian distilled options have added subtle characteristics, and we've featured them in a few of the recipes, to assist in giving potency to the drink.

WHISKY To create whisky (or whiskey, the spelling depends on its origin), grains such as barley, rye, corn and wheat are fermented and distilled. There are several categories of whisky, with strict regulations regarding classification, and they include single malt, blended Scotch, Irish, Canadian, bourbon and spiced. Flavours are dramatically affected by alterations at each level of production, from the makeup of the mash for fermentation, the type of yeast used and the style of still and distillation process, to the length of aging and the type of barrel used. Ensure that your bar has Scotch (at least one less expensive blend and, if you like, a peaty single malt too), plus a bottle of rye whisky. From there, explore the endless list of great options, like bourbon (often sweeter), unaged and spiced whiskies.

Up Your Game

⤚⊙ ⊙⤙

Add some of these less essential but truly fantastic bottles to your cabinet, plus the many more listed within these pages:

ABSINTHE, ALLSPICE DRAM, AMARO, APEROL, AQUAVIT, BRANDY, CHACHAÇA, CAMPARI, CHARTREUSE, CHERRY HEERING, CYNAR, EAU-DE-VIE, ELDERFLOWER LIQUEUR, FALERNUM, FERNET, LILLET, MARASCHINO, MEZCAL, PIMM'S, PISCO, SHERRY, STREGA, TEQUILA

COUPE

MARTINI

CHAMPAGNE FLUTE

WINE

SHOT

HIGHBALL

APERITIF

GLASSWARE

TIKI

OLD-FASHIONED

JULEP

MUG

HEAT PROOF GLASS

COLLINS

DOUBLE OLD-FASHIONED

COAST
to
COAST
to
COAST

*C*HEFS AND AUTHORS across the country have contemplated the conundrum of Canadian cuisine for well over a century, and we have found ourselves heading down a similar path. What makes a drink Canadian? What makes a *Canadian* Canadian? Someone in Newfoundland might have a very different answer from someone in Quebec or Alberta. Canada is an enormous country with a vibrant history and a multitude of socio-cultural influences. It's too complicated to pinpoint any single unifying factor that qualifies one as Canadian (a love of maple syrup? beer? hockey? politeness?). Attempting to reel in and label its people and flavours under the umbrella term *Canadian* seems arbitrary if not impossible. We know there are a variety of elements that make up our culture; in a way, being Canadian is a celebration of all of them. Luckily for us, stirred or shaken, our rich history and icons, ingredients and inspirations blend together seamlessly, to make an exquisite, well-balanced cocktail. Here is our collection of Canadian-style drinks—cocktails that don't represent just one specific region (those recipes come later) but encapsulate the broad spectrum that is Canada. >

Going back to what comes to mind when you think of Canadian drinks, good old Canadian whisky—rye whisky, that is—is a liquor front-runner. It's a spirit that Canadians are both famous and notorious for, thanks to its inclusion in vintage classic cocktails and because of our bootlegging history. The first cocktail in this book is made with our beloved Canadian whisky and takes its roots from a historical recipe from the comprehensive cocktail book, *Bottoms Up*.

THE CANADIAN

We have Ted Saucier to thank for this beauty of a cocktail. He included a recipe from J.H. Campbell in *Bottoms Up*. In that version, maple syrup is used, but ours is different; it could be likened more to a classic Old-Fashioned, made with maple sugar candy in place of a sugar cube.

1 small maple leaf sugar candy, no larger than 1 inch in diameter

2 dashes Bittered Sling Kensington Dry Aromatic bitters or Angostura bitters

1 large ice cube

2 oz Canadian rye whisky, such as Alberta Premium Dark Horse

Handful of ice cubes

1 lemon peel strip

Cut maple leaf in half. Place one half into an old-fashioned glass. Add bitters. Muddle into a paste. Add large ice cube to old-fashioned glass along with paste. Pour in whisky. Pull a long strip of lemon peel over the glass, releasing oils into cocktail. Gently pinch, peel side out, misting oils over surface of the drink. Rub peel around the outside rim of the glass, then add.

Makes 1 drink

Bottoms Up

Ted Saucier was a Waldorf Astoria Hotel publicist who compiled *Bottoms Up*, published in 1951. In it, you'll find 200 drink recipes of that era and earlier, amid pin-up girl illustrations. Saucier is Canadian born but earned his reputation in America, where he spent most of his life. His fondness for his birthplace is evident by the Canadian-centric recipes peppered throughout *Bottoms Up*. In recent years, bartenders have revisited and updated Saucier's recipes, making way for the resurgence in drinks like The Last Word and Hotel Georgia—when in Vancouver, be sure to pop in to the Rosewood Hotel Georgia to enjoy a version of this classic. We had a perfect one there at Hawksworth Restaurant.

Our next recipe also comes from the history books, thanks to another Canadian author with a fondness for brown spirits. Stephen Leacock is well known for his political satire and eloquent yet quirky humour. He was a proud anti-prohibitionist and wrote frequently on the subject of alcohol. Rooting through a collection of pieces entitled *Wet Wit and Dry Humour*, published in 1931, we came across his ingredient list for a Hot Toddy.

HOT TODDY

This classic cocktail has no doubt helped many Canucks combat our cold northern winters. Leacock's instructions are not exact, but a Hot Toddy is rarely prepared precisely anyhow. So we've mixed up our ideal winter warmer based on his witty description:

I remember, too, that in the old times in the winter evenings we used to sit around the fire in one another's houses smoking and drinking hot toddy. No doubt you remember the awful stuff. We generally used to make ours with Bourbon whiskey and hot water, with just a dash of rum, with half a dozen lumps of white sugar in it, and with nutmeg powdered over the top. I think we used to put a curled slice of lemon peel into the rotten stuff and then served it in a tall tumbler with a long spoon in it. We used to sit and sup this beastly mixture all evening and carry on a perfectly aimless conversation with no selected subject of discussion, and with absolutely no attempt to improve our minds at all.

—*The Garden of Folly*, 1924

1 thin lemon wedge

3 whole cloves

1 tsp granulated sugar or 1 sugar cube

1 oz bourbon

½ oz allspice dram

4 oz boiling hot water

1 long cinnamon stick

Stud lemon wedge with cloves. Place sugar into a warmed heatproof glass or mug. Add bourbon and allspice dram. Pour in boiling hot water. Carefully stir with cinnamon stick or a long spoon until sugar is dissolved. Gently squeeze in juice from studded lemon wedge, then carefully add.

Makes 1 drink

BOTTLE BASICS
Allspice dram is a rum-based liqueur infused with allspice berries. St. Elizabeth allspice dram and Bitter Truth pimento dram are two of the best and most well-known brands on the market. If you don't have allspice dram, use a combination of ¼ oz dark rum plus 3 dashes Angostura bitters in its place.

The Caesar is a quintessential Canadian drink. As with many other cocktails, similar versions with varying names have appeared on menus across North America. The classic Canadian Caesar that we know today, however, was titled and popularized by barman Walter Chell in Calgary in 1969. Our consistent complaint when travelling is that you just can't get a good Caesar outside Canada, and sometimes a Bloody Mary (*sans* rimmer and clam juice) just won't do. We feel so patriotic about this drink that we've included duelling Caesar variations here (plus a couple more elsewhere in the book).

THE GREAT WHITE CAESAR

Here's a riff on this classic drink tailored to gardeners and DIY-ers. We've used homemade rimmer and Tomato-Clam Juice—made with Canadian clams and super sweet, juicy, Great White tomatoes—but store-bought juice and rimmer will also do the trick.

Lovage-Salt Rimmer or celery salt
1 lime or lemon wedge
Handful of ice cubes
1 ½ oz vodka
2 dashes hot sauce, preferably green or Cholula
1 dash Worcestershire sauce
Generous grinding black pepper
4 to 6 oz chilled Tomato-Clam Juice (page 193)
Half lime or lemon wheel, for garnish
1 sprig of lovage or cilantro, for garnish

Place rimmer on a small plate. Moisten the rim of a large highball or pint glass with lime wedge. Turn the outside rim of the glass in rimmer. Fill glass with ice. Pour in vodka. Add hot sauce and Worcestershire. Sprinkle with pepper and squeeze in juice from lime wedge. Top with Tomato-Clam Juice. Stir to mix and chill drink. Taste and adjust flavouring to your liking. Garnish with half lime wheel.

Makes 1 drink

> *Lovage-Salt Rimmer* <

Preheat the oven to 200°F. Lightly pound ½ cup finely chopped lovage (see page 198) or cilantro leaves (1 small bunch) with ½ cup coarse kosher salt using a mortar and pestle. Spread out over a large parchment-lined baking sheet. Bake until herbs are very dry and brittle, 30 to 60 minutes. Remove from oven and allow to cool completely. Rimmer will keep well in a sealed container at room temperature for up to 6 months. Makes $^2/_3$ cup rimmer

EAST–MEETS–WEST COAST CAESAR

One of our all-time favourite cocktail-and-food pairings is a Caesar served alongside fresh seafood. So we've combined the best of both worlds by creating this classic cocktail, loaded with fresh Canadian seafood garnishes! The result? The perfect hair-of-the-dog cocktail that's a meal in itself.

Dulse-Salt Rimmer
1 lemon or lime
Handful of ice cubes
1½ oz vodka
1 tsp freshly grated horseradish
2 dashes hot sauce, preferably Cholula
2 dashes Worcestershire sauce
Generous grinding black pepper
4 to 6 oz chilled Tomato-Clam Juice (page 193), preferably using red tomatoes
1 cooked large BC shrimp, peeled and deveined, tail-on, for garnish
1 steamed clam and/or 1 fresh Canadian East or West Coast oyster, for garnish (see shucking tip, page 194) (optional)

Place rimmer on a small plate. Cut 2 lemon wedges, one of them large. Use large lemon wedge to moisten the rim of a large highball or pint glass. Turn the outside rim of the glass in rimmer. Fill glass with ice. Pour in vodka. Add horseradish, hot sauce and Worcestershire. Sprinkle with pepper and squeeze in juice from large lemon wedge. Top with Tomato-Clam Juice. Stir to mix and chill drink. Taste and adjust seasoning to your liking. Skewer shrimp and clam, if using. Garnish Caesar with a lemon wedge, seafood skewer and a freshly shucked oyster, if using, balanced over the ice.
Makes 1 drink

> *Dulse-Salt Rimmer* <

Dulse is a red-tinged dark purple seaweed that grows on rocks on the shorelines of the Atlantic and Pacific Oceans. It's hugely popular among Maritimers as a sea-vegetable snack. It carries intense umami taste that's also salty and earthy and sings of sea flavour, making it an excellent base for a Caesar rimmer. We would like to give a shout out to Patrick McMurray's The Ceili Cottage in Toronto, the place where we first tried it in a Caesar. To make our dulse rimmer simply place ½ cup coarsely broken dulse and 1 Tbsp coarse kosher salt in a spice or coffee grinder. Pulse until broken down. Add another 1 Tbsp salt. Pulse just to mix. Rimmer will keep well in a sealed container at room temperature for up to 2 months. Makes 2 Tbsp rimmer

En Garde: EAST—MEETS—WEST COAST CAESAR (left) *vs.* THE GREAT WHITE CAESAR

The word *terroir* contains the French root *terre*, meaning "land" or "earth." Within the context of food and drink, terroir often refers to flavours that are influenced by and that reflect elements of the land from which they come. Beyond enjoying terroir traditionally through food and wine, we find ourselves experiencing and using it in spirits and cocktails, in order to give them a distinctive and localized taste. There are many manufacturers, old and new, that take advantage of homegrown, regionally specific ingredients and flavours in Canada, capturing the spirits and essence of the areas where they are produced. Gin is a prime example of a spirit that can clearly illustrate Canadian terroir. Here is a classic cocktail to showcase the intricacies of this spirit beautifully.

GIN & TONIC

This simple drink is often taken for granted. You can slap one together or, with careful consideration, you can put together a truly solid drink. The key is good technique and allowing the nuances of the gin you've selected to shine through.

Handful of ice cubes
1 ½ to 2 oz gin
¾ oz Tonic Syrup (page 186)
3 oz chilled club soda
1 lime wedge

Add gin to an ice-filled chilled old-fashioned glass. Add Tonic Syrup. Top with soda. Squeeze in juice from lime wedge. Stir to incorporate.
Makes 1 drink

CLASSIC SHORTCUT
If you don't have homemade, simply omit the Tonic Syrup
and soda combo and use 4 to 6 oz store-bought tonic water instead.

Canadian Gin

⊷═◉ ◉═⊷

Gin offers a great opportunity for distillers to showcase their own creative blends, often highlighting regional flavours and distinctly local ingredients. Apart from careful manipulation and the selection of botanicals, gin is also influenced by subtle variables such as the source of water or the type of juniper used.

BEYOND THE TRADITIONAL

These quality gins include unusual additions reflecting Canadian terroir:

Saskatchewan
- Silver Sperling Distillery, Holy Spirits Gin uses bi-product from the brewing process of Slow Pub and neighbouring pubs to create the moonshine-esque spirit base.

Ontario
- Dillon's Small Batch Distillers, Unfiltered Gin 22 uses a grape spirit base with the fruit being sourced from the Niagara wine region.

Quebec
- Domaine Pinnacle Microdistillerie, Ungava Premium Dry Gin utilizes botanicals native to Quebec's Ungava region, including nordic juniper, arctic blend, Labrador tea, crowberry, cloudberry and wild rose hips.

New Brunswick
- Distillerie Fils du Roy, Gin Thuya features eastern white cedar, the same tree that staved off scurvy for early settlers along the Acadian coast, *Thuja occidentalis*.

Yukon Territory
- Yukon Shine Distillery, AuraGin uses Yukon gold potatoes for its base spirit and is also filtered through a mix of charcoal and actual Yukon gold.

CLASSIC-STYLE

Here are some homegrown gems:

British Columbia
- Dubh Glas Distillery, Noteworthy Gin
- The Yaletown Distilling Company, Yaletown Gin
- Victoria Spirits, Victoria Gin
- Okanagan Spirits, Gin
- Long Table Distillery, London dry gin

Alberta
- Eau Claire Distillery, Parlour Gin

Ontario
- Georgian Bay Gin, Georgian Bay Gin
- Toronto Distillery Co. Limited, J.R.'s Dry Organic Canadian Gin
- 66 Gilead Distillery, Loyalist Gin

Prince Edward Island
- Prince Edward Distillery, Prince Edward Artisan Distilled Gin

All too often fruit liqueurs get a bad reputation for being cloyingly sweet or artificially flavoured. While travelling across Canada, we were delighted to discover so many beautifully crafted liqueurs prepared from fresh, regionally grown fruits. Many Canadian producers take advantage of the fruit from their own land or overflow from neighbouring farms and orchards. The results are liqueurs packed with terroir, exhibiting subtle differences from region to region and highlighting the richness and nuances, much the same way wine does.

KIR & KIR ROYALE

We love a Kir (a classic French aperitif) and a Kir Royale (made with bubbly) for their versatility, and especially because they make for a beautiful vessel to showcase Canadian wines and Crème de Cassis liqueur. It's the kind of drink that doesn't really require a recipe, only a few guidelines. Mix and match your favourites and adjust amounts to your taste.

¾ oz Crème de Cassis
4 ½ oz chilled dry white wine, such as
    Sauvignon Blanc or unoaked Chardonnay,
    or dry sparkling wine

Add Crème de Cassis to a wine glass, champagne flute or coupe glass. Top with wine for a Kir or sparkling wine for a Kir Royale. Every cassis boasts different viscosity, sweetness and flavours, so taste and adjust cassis or wine to your liking.
Makes 1 drink

Canadian Crème de Cassis

—✦—❦—✦—

Cassis is French for blackcurrant. The delectable velvety liqueur that bears the name Crème de Cassis is most commonly associated with France. When Jacques Cartier arrived, he had high hopes that New France could be a successful wine region. These were reinforced when he stumbled upon an island in the St. Lawrence covered with wild grapes, which he dubbed Île de Bacchus, after the notorious god of wine. Among those grapes, which sadly do not make the best wines, he probably saw blackcurrants too. The agriculturally rich Île d'Orléans (as Île de Bacchus was renamed) is rife with them. So it's no surprise that the island is home to one of our favourite Crèmes de Cassis, produced by Cassis Monna & Filles. While wine may have been tougher to master in New France, the French tradition of making Crème de Cassis took hold in Quebec and is now common across the country.

CANADIAN CRÈME DE CASSIS LIQUEURS

Here are some of our favourite Crèmes de Cassis:

British Columbia
- Odd Society Spirits, Crème de Cassis
- Okanagan Spirits, Blackcurrant Liqueur

Alberta
- Field Stone fruit wines, Black Currant Dessert Wine

Quebec
- Mondia Alliance, L'Orléane Cassis de L'Île d'Orléans, Crème de Cassis
- Cassis Monna & Filles, Crème de Cassis

New Brunswick
- Happy Knight, Crème de Cassis

Prince Edward Island
- Rossignol Estate Winery, Crème de Cassis

Newfoundland
- Rodrigues Winery, Blackcurrant Liqueur

OTHER FRUIT LIQUEURS

Experiment with Kir by using fruit liqueur in place of Crème de Cassis. Here are some standouts:

British Columbia
- Okanagan Spirits, Sea Buckthorn Liqueur

Saskatchewan
- LB Distillers, Saskatoon Liqueur or Haskap (blue honeysuckle) Liqueur

Quebec
- Cidrerie et Vergers Pedneault, Crème de Petites Poire, Saskatoonberry Liquor

New Brunswick
- Distillerie Fils du Roy, Le Souverain Bleu

Nova Scotia
- Ironworks Distillery, Saskatoon Berry Liqueur or Rhubarb Esprit

From the first peek of rhubarb above the frosty soil to the last bites of crisp apples and juicy pears, fresh produce is something that all Canadians greet with anticipation. The bright taste of local, in-season fruit makes waiting out the wintery months worthwhile. Fruit ripe for the picking can be eaten straight out of hand, served between buttery pie crusts, preserved in jams and jellies and, of course, used to infuse liquids such as alcohol or vinegar, muddled in cocktails or used as a garnish.

SOUR SLUSH

Making an old-fashioned shrub, or drinking vinegar, is a fantastic way to draw out and preserve fresh fruit flavour. Experiment with what you have on hand. Sweetened and infused vinegar can be enjoyed over ice, lengthened with soda or mixed with alcohol to form delightful and complex cocktails.

We've blended our sweet-sour fruit shrub with your favourite spirit and lots of ice to create a whimsical summer slushy. It's a flexible recipe that is satisfying without alcohol too. Simply replace the booze with water.

2 cups crushed ice	Pulse crushed ice in a blender. With motor running, pour shrub, then gin, through hole in lid. Scrape down sides of blender, then continue blending until shaved ice forms. Serve in a julep cup or a tin mug or jar.
2 oz Canadian Fruit Shrub	
2 oz gin, vodka or rum	
	Makes 1 drink

> *Canadian Fruit Shrub* <

¾ cup coarsely chopped rhubarb, peaches, wild strawberries, cherries or pricked blueberries or halved Concord grapes

½ cup granulated sugar
²/₃ cup white wine vinegar or champagne vinegar
½ cup water

Place fruit in a resealable container. Pour sugar overtop. Seal container and shake. Refrigerate for 24 hours, shaking occasionally, to allow fruit to macerate and sugar to pull out fruit juices. Turn fruit and sugar into a saucepan. Pour in vinegar and water. Warm over medium heat until fruit softens slightly, 7 to 9 minutes (rhubarb will take a little longer). Remove from heat and let cool completely. Strain liquid through a large funnel lined with several layers of cheesecloth into a resealable container. Squeeze out any excess juices. Discard solids. Shrub will keep well, sealed and refrigerated, for at least 1 month. Makes 12 oz (1 ½ cups), for 6 slushes

Shrub on Ice: SOUR SLUSH

Cocktails have a history of adopting namesakes or being dedications to persons, places and things. For this book, we've taken the opportunity to emphasize inspiration from this great land we live in, as have many of our featured bartenders. Our next cocktail is a perfect example of just that; it's inspired by a Canadian road trip pastime. Highway pit stops are a must when travelling Canada, given the vast spaces and long stretches between cities. They're a chance to stretch your legs, grab a snack, refuel and recharge with a hot coffee. Here's a cocktail for you to enjoy as you sit back and take a trans-Canada-cocktail journey with us.

THE DOUBLE DOUBLE

Ask any Canadian what a double double is and you'll get a description of a sweet, creamy coffee that Canucks "always have time for." Although the double double—coffee with two creams and two sugars—isn't technically on the Tim Hortons menu, it's become synonymous with the brand. We couldn't resist making a nighttime counterpart to the popular coffee order. We initially envisioned an equal-parts drink—two shots whisky and two shots Kahlúa—but we realized it's just not a double double without all that creamy goodness, so we incorporated whisky cream liqueur.

1 ½ oz Canadian whisky, such as
   Forty Creek Barrel Select
¾ oz Kahlúa
¾ oz Forty Creek Cream Liquor
1 dash Angostura bitters
Handful of ice cubes
Small pinch finely ground espresso, for garnish

Pour all ingredients except ice and espresso into a mixing glass. Add ice and stir until chilled. Strain through a julep strainer into a chilled mug or glass. Sprinkle with espresso to garnish. Serve with a coffee stir stick, if you like.
Makes 1 drink

FORTY CREEK

You can use other types of whisky, but we love that Forty Creek Distillery is near Hamilton, Ontario, the city where the first Tim Hortons coffee shop opened, in 1964.
Plus, they make great whisky!

THE CANADIAN COCKTAIL ADVENTURE

The recipes in this last section highlight how Canadian cocktails can be just as diverse and eclectic as our history, culture, landscape and ingredients. You may find that not all ingredients are readily available everywhere in Canada, but each of these drinks can be prepared regardless of where you live. If a recipe calls for cloudberry liqueur or sea buckthorn or Canadian sake but you don't have it on hand, get creative and try out what is nearest and dearest to you. And if you can't make it to the barstools to sit across from the extraordinarily talented bartenders featured in this book, go ahead and try out their recipes for friends at your own home bar. Our field guide, whether it's in your suitcase or on your bookcase, will lead you down the path to enjoy a truly Canadian cocktail adventure.

The Bush Pilot

(pg 176)

Saucier's Seigniory Special

(pg 127)

Chinook Sangria

(pg 71)

The Corroded Nail

(pg 159)

The Flatlander's Fizz

(pg 82)

The

WEST

RECIPES IN THIS SECTION:

JACK WITH ONE EYE

SEA ISLAND ICED TEA

SASKATOON JULEP

CANADIAN WINTER'S PUNCH

THE OENOPHILE

ROCKET RICHARDONNAY

OGOPOGO SOUR

EL CAMINO 2.0

BOB & DOUG'S STRANGE BREW

SUNKEN PORT

WHAT'S UP, DOC?

THE EMPEROR

SMOKY LAKE OLD-FASHIONED

CAMPFIRE FLIP

BUTCHART GARDEN SWIZZLE

With over two dozen distilleries, more than fifty breweries and brewpubs, a handful of burgeoning cider makers and meaderies, groundbreaking sake producers and, to top that all off, one of the world's most beautiful winemaking regions, British Columbia is a cocktail mecca—and a perfect place for us to embark on our self-guided cocktail-tasting tour. To scout for the finest cocktails to include in this chapter, we flew to Vancouver and then travelled to Vancouver Island and the Okanagan.

The first friend we made on our cocktail pilgrimage was essential in steering us in the right direction. Upon arriving at Opus Hotel in Vancouver's Yaletown, we checked our bags and promptly went to the hotel bar, La Pentola, to meet head bartender Martin Corriveau and enjoy our first BC cocktails. After nerding out over ice, trying samples of his fantastic house-made falernum and enjoying spirits that aren't currently sold back home in Ontario, we tried a bottled, fizzy Corpse Reviver #2 and a gorgeous, smoky mezcal drink. Martin then proceeded to pull out a map of downtown Vancouver and jot down the names and locations of his favourite cocktail bars as other patrons enthusiastically joined in with their top picks. We had already arrived with a fully plotted taste trail, but this

affirmed our picks and topped us up with a couple more. And, we felt, we were on to something: when travelling, talk to your bartenders and ask them where they love to go.

The next day, we water-taxied over to Granville Island to fuel up at the market. We picked up a smorgasbord-style lunch that included vegetarian salads, a snowy-rind goat's milk wheel, Terra Breads' crusty baguette and Oyama Sausage Co. charcuterie (where they offer cured meats with cocktail pairing suggestions). We dropped by Artisan SakeMaker for a lovely tasting. Check out Vancouver cocktail icon and bitters maker Lauren Mote's salute to this sake maker in her cocktail The Emperor (page 56).

The following days and nights were a dazzling dream-like state of eating and drinking. We met some of Canada's most friendly and innovative bartenders and were blown away with the consistent quality of our cocktail experiences. Our list of must-try joints kept expanding, especially when Thor Paulson, an exceptional bartender at The Diamond, took the time to note his A-list spots on a bar coaster. His list, like most, included L'Abattoir, which was across the street, in Gastown. Along with so many other spots in Vancouver, they take special care there in pairing food with cocktails. Victoria enjoyed an otherworldly Dungeness crab appetizer with a wonderful watermelon- and tequila-based cocktail, the El Camino 2.0. Head barman Shaun Layton shared that recipe so it can be replicated at home (see page 50).

Vancouver's vibrant bar community is educated and artful, always demonstrating a firm grasp of refined technique. Thoughtful drinks are calculated—methodically incorporating the overall elements and quality of ingredients—to yield spectacular results. Although our visit and our lists could go on and on, we said goodbye to Vancouver on a breathtaking ferry ride as we headed to Victoria, and the cleansing sea air refreshed and revived us from our noble attempt to try every cocktail bar in Vancouver.

Once we checked into the Magnolia Hotel in Victoria, we decided to put our "get advice at the bar" theory to the test, hoping to duplicate the success we had in Vancouver. Downstairs at the Catalano Restaurant & Cicchetti Bar, we had a lively chat with the bartender. Once again, we were set on the right path. At our next stop, Veneto Tapa Lounge, we met bartenders Simon Ogden and Josh Boudreau and tried an arguably afternoon-appropriate cocktail, the What's Up, Doc? (page 54). The following night we headed to Clive's Classic Lounge to chat with

executive barkeep Katie McDonald. The most memorable part of our visit was transporting Katie's enoki-infusion to another local bar as part of a "boomerang" challenge. The defending bartender, Brant Porter over at Little Jumbo, didn't flinch and within moments created a Martinez-inspired cocktail. This was one small insight into the close-knit community in Victoria and demonstrates how healthy competition is a great way to push each other creatively and, ultimately, to imagine and transform first-class cocktails. This sense of community is one of the reasons Victoria is well respected within the international cocktail scene.

On our way off the island we paid a visit to Victoria Spirits distillery. Its gin was one of the first Canadian craft gins we found in Ontario. It was fun to see the still first-hand, inhale the wonderful aromas from the gin-making process and check out the distillery's surreal forest setting, located as it is down the road from the Butchart Gardens. The excursion was an afternoon of stunning sensory overload and the inspiration for our Butchart Garden Swizzle (page 61).

Painterly views, blissful temperatures and sublime landscapes became common themes for the next days of travel as we made our way through southern

British Columbia, headed to the Okanagan Valley. Amid the driving and ferry rides, we had a welcome reprieve with a home-cooked meal with our publisher, Robert—all the dishes he prepared were from *Jerusalem*, the cookbook by Yotam Ottolenghi and Sami Tamimi. Now that we were officially well nourished and revitalized, we prepared ourselves for some serious mountain driving. After great deliberation, we decided on a route—the Crowsnest Highway, rather than the Coquihalla. We have no regrets, but we probably do have a few more bottles of wine than we would otherwise, that we snagged from the wonderful Forbidden Fruit Winery in Cawston and Road 13 Vineyards in Oliver. We also scooped up some of the first cherries of the season at a roadside stand in Osoyoos before continuing north to our Okanagan home base of Kelowna.

We reached Kelowna in time to catch a gorgeous sunset, stow away our recently acquired wines and make our dinner reservation at RauDZ Regional Table. If you don't have time to drive around and tour the various regions and wineries, dining at RauDZ is a great way to experience the area's best. The local-focused establishment has a constantly evolving menu that showcases the bounty of the area with an extensive wine list and phenomenal, creative cocktails (see Micah Jensen's Rocket Richardonnay, page 47).

With the area's incredible produce and abundance of orchards, it is no surprise that there are several distilleries in the Okanagan and some of the tastiest spirits and liqueurs this country produces. Bartenders all over the west reach for bottles from the Okanagan. We loved our visit to Maple Leaf Spirits, where we experienced a thorough tasting. At Okanagan Spirits Craft Distillery we also had the chance to taste our way through its large roster and saw staff distilling the spirit base for nearby Gray Monk Estate Winery's port-style Odyssey III. Katie McDonald calls for this in her Sunken Port (page 53).

It was hard to leave, but with a few bottles from La Frenz Winery, a delectable charcuterie spread from Salted Brick and a small basket of fresh fruit, we were able to preserve a little Okanagan flavour for our next journey.

Despite all our tasting experiences, adventures never seem to satiate the wanderlust. We are looking forward to plotting our next trips. We long to try more of what Western Canada has to offer. Hopefully, our trip tales are getting your taste buds buzzing too. In the coming pages, you'll find recipes to take you on a journey through Western Canada while sipping from the comfort of your armchair.

JACK WITH ONE EYE

We've dedicated this boozy sipper to the cult classic television show *Twin Peaks*. Early in the series, some of the characters cross the border into western Canada and head to a casino and brothel called One Eyed Jacks. We were thrilled to include several nods to flavour mentions in that episode, after discovering they worked wonderfully together in a spirit-forward cocktail.

1 ½ oz bourbon or Canadian whisky

1 oz cold- or French-pressed good-quality brewed coffee, chilled

½ oz Cointreau or Triple Sec

1 barspoon maraschino cherry juice or cherry liqueur

1 dash mole bitters

Handful of ice cubes

1 large ice cube

1 maraschino cherry, preferably with a stem

Pour all ingredients except ice and cherry into a mixing glass. Add handful of ice cubes and stir until chilled. Strain through a julep strainer over large ice cube in a chilled old-fashioned glass. Serve with a skewered cherry.

Makes 1 drink

CHEEKY GARNISH

Please hard-core fans by tying the maraschino cherry stem
into a knot before garnishing.

SEA ISLAND ICED TEA

JUSTIN TAYLOR uprooted from Toronto and moved to Vancouver, where he now oversees both Boulevard Kitchen & Oyster Bar and Gerard Lounge in the prestigious Sutton Place Hotel. He names this drink after the island location of the Vancouver International Airport, the place where he felt instantly welcome in the West. For ingredients he looked to the best his newly adopted province has to offer, from Fraser Valley cranberries to the spirits and liqueurs of the Okanagan, and lemon juice from Vancouver Island lemon trees. Justin calls for his favourite local brands, but this drink works well with substitutions too.

3 oz brewed Tea Leaves jasmine green tea,
    cooled
1 ½ oz Okanagan Spirits Aquavitus Aquavit
½ oz Okanagan Spirits Sea Buckthorn Liqueur
½ oz freshly squeezed lemon juice
½ oz unsweetened cranberry juice,
    such as Bremner's
½ oz Ginger-Infused Honey Syrup
2 large handfuls of ice cubes

Pour all ingredients except ice into a cocktail shaker. Add first handful of ice. Shake to incorporate ingredients, 10 seconds. Strain through a Hawthorne strainer into an ice-filled collins glass.
Makes 1 drink

> *Ginger-Infused Honey Syrup* <

Bring ½ cup wildflower honey, preferably Honeybee Centre, ½ cup water and 2 Tbsp grated fresh ginger to a boil in a small saucepan. Simmer, stirring occasionally, over medium-low heat for 10 minutes. Remove from heat, chill and strain into a sterilized jar. Syrup will keep, sealed and refrigerated, for 2 weeks. Makes 8 oz (1 cup), for 16 drinks

SASKATOON JULEP

NATE CAUDLE worked at some of Victoria's best restaurants before becoming head bartender at Little Jumbo where you can enjoy wildly inventive cocktails and excellent versions of classics. This take on a Julep pays tribute to Nate's Prairie roots and uses Saskatoon berry liqueur. We used store-bought liqueur from LB Distillers (made in Saskatoon) to stir up this sweet and minty treat. In Nate's book *Cocktail Culture*, co-written with Shawn Soole (owner of Little Jumbo), you can find his recipe for a delicious homemade Saskatoon berry liqueur.

8 to 10 fresh mint leaves, plus 1 sprig, for garnish
Crushed ice
1 ½ oz Forty Creek Barrel Select Whisky
1 oz Saskatoon berry liqueur
½ oz Simple Syrup (page 182)
Icing sugar, for garnish

Pour all ingredients except garnishes into a chilled old-fashioned glass. Stir vigorously until flavours infuse and mixture is chilled. Garnish with mint sprig sprinkled with icing sugar.
Makes 1 drink

CANADIAN WINTER'S PUNCH

DAVID WOLOWIDNYK is a champion in bartending competitions and also when it comes to whirlwind cocktail travels, putting our itineraries to shame—he told us he once visited sixty-five New York bars in a mere six days. This thoroughness comes as no surprise: David is renowned in Vancouver for his dedication and knowledge in the art of drink. He's worked at West for years and is currently working on opening his own place too. His Winter's Punch is inspired by Jerry Thomas's Canadian Punch.

1 orange
1 lemon
8-cup sterilized jar
1 cinnamon stick
1 vanilla bean, scored
½ whole nutmeg, crushed in a mortar and pestle
1 Tbsp whole allspice
4 cups Canadian rye whisky
1 cup dark rum
4 lemons, sliced and seeded
1 peeled fresh pineapple, sliced
6 cups Chilled Earl Grey Tea
1 large block of ice that fits a punch bowl

Using a peeler, pull the full peel from orange and lemon, removing any pith. Add both to jar. Add spices, vanilla, then whisky and rum. Infuse for 2 days. Strain through a coffee filter–lined funnel into a punch bowl to remove any particles. Add sliced lemons and pineapple. Let infuse for 8 hours. Add tea, then block of ice, and serve.

Makes 28 drinks

> *Chilled Earl Grey Tea* <

Bring 8 cups water to a boil. Place 2 Tbsp Earl Grey tea leaves in a fine-mesh strainer. Rinse with 1 cup boiling water, discarding the water. Place rinsed tea leaves in a large heatproof receptacle that can easily be used to pour. Pour remaining 7 cups boiling water overtop. Let steep for exactly 3 minutes. Fine strain 6 cups brewed tea into a large measuring cup with a spout, leaving tea leaves and any bits behind. Stir 1 cup granulated sugar into strained tea. Let cool completely. Makes 6 cups

THE OENOPHILE

Jay Jones, once named GQ's Most Imaginative Bartender of the year (2012), has a diverse resumé. He has tended bars at West and Blackbird Public House, and heads up the drinks program for the Vancouver Canucks. He is a champion of locally crafted goods. His take on Sangria, he says, "bridges the gap between wine and cocktails." The combination of bitters adds savoury structure and a peppery boost. Jay notes that the absence of ice is key to exhibiting the drink's natural texture and richness while allowing the drink to gently warm in the glass, revealing more complexities as it's enjoyed.

2 cups LaStella Fortissimo

3 ½ oz Okanagan Spirits Old Italian
   Prune Brandy Eau de Vie

1 ¾ oz Giffard Abricot de Roussillon

21 dashes Bittered Sling Denman bitters

14 dashes Bittered Sling Cascade Celery bitters

Stir all ingredients together in a large pitcher. Pour through a funnel into a large resealable bottle, such as a 750 mL wine bottle. Refrigerate until chilled to 56°F. Pour each serving into a wine glass, preferably crystal claret.

Makes 5 drinks

SUBSTITUTIONS

If you're unable to get these specific ingredients, Jay recommends using any premium full-bodied red wine and/or apricot liqueur and quality Spanish brandy in place of the prune brandy.

ROCKET RICHARDONNAY

Although MICAH JENSEN lived and worked in Vancouver for years, his connection to and knowledge of his hometown of Kelowna and the surrounding Okanagan region help make his cocktail list personal and comprehensive. He practises a range of cocktail styles—which style depends on where he's working. At RauDZ Regional Table, where he developed this wine-spiked twist on a vesper, he is dedicated to field-to-glass-style drinks. It's prepared with primarily Canadian ingredients and it's dedicated to Canadian hockey hero Maurice "the Rocket" Richard.

1 oz Spirit Bear Vodka
1 oz Okanagan Spirits Gin
2 oz Chardonnay-Maple Reduction
1 lemon peel strip
Handful of ice cubes
1 edible flower, for garnish (optional)

Pour all ingredients except ice and garnish into a mixing glass, including lemon peel. Add ice and stir until ice cold. Double strain through a julep strainer and a fine-mesh strainer into a chilled coupe glass. Garnish with edible flower, if you like.

Makes 1 drink

> *Chardonnay-Maple Reduction* <

Pour 1 bottle (750 mL) Canadian Chardonnay, such as Red Rooster, into a small saucepan. Set over high heat. Bring to a boil, then let vigorously boil for 2 to 3 minutes until reduced by about one-third. Stir in ¾ cup + 2 Tbsp maple syrup, preferably Canadian No. 1. Remove from heat and let cool completely. Pour into a sterilized jar. Reduction will keep well, sealed and refrigerated, for 1 week. Makes 30 oz (3 ½ cups), for more than a dozen drinks

OGOPOGO SOUR

The Okanagan Valley feels like a strange Eden—a lush landscape of vineyards and orchards in the middle of desert mountains that are lightly covered with sagebrush. Along with the Similkameen and Kootenay Valleys, the Okanagan supplies Canada with 60% of the country's cherries. It seemed fitting to dedicate this frothy coupe to Ogopogo, the legendary Okanagan Lake sea monster, since it's inspired by her fruitful home. The Scotch is a nod to Ogopogo's cousin, the Loch Ness Monster; the Scotch adds character while enhancing the balance of tangy lemon and nutty orgeat. This riff on a classic Sour is a thirst-quencher for sipping on those hot, dry Okanagan afternoons.

¾ oz or 1 small egg white

¾ oz kirsch, such as Maple Leaf Spirits
　　Canadian Kirsch

¾ oz cherry liqueur

¾ oz freshly squeezed lemon juice

¼ oz Scotch

¼ oz orgeat

Large handful of ice cubes

3 to 4 drops Bittered Sling Suius Cherry bitters
　　or Angostura bitters

1 fresh cherry or homemade cocktail cherry
　　(page 188), for garnish

Pour all ingredients except ice, bitters and garnish into a cocktail shaker. Shake until incorporated and frothy. Add ice and shake until chilled. Double strain through a Hawthorne strainer and a fine-mesh strainer into a chilled coupe glass. Dot bitters over surface of the drink, in an up-and-down pattern. Use a straw to connect the dots and create a design (maybe an Ogopogo-shaped one). Garnish with cherry.

Makes 1 drink

A WEE DRAM

Despite the small amount of Scotch used in this drink, its flavour really shines through.
For the best results, choose a type (peaty or non) that you enjoy drinking on its own.

EL CAMINO 2.0

SHAUN LAYTON is much loved and highly respected by the bartending community and patrons alike. Take a seat across from him at the bar and he'll reveal his knowledge and devotion to the topic of drinks while making you feel right at home. This recipe is one of his classics revised as a 2.0 version, and it's easy to see why this sparkling watermelon-infused tequila drink is a mainstay on his menu.

Mild tasting salt, such as fleur de sel
    or Maldon
1 lime
1 long very thin watermelon slice
Crushed ice
2 oz Watermelon and Campari–Infused Tequila
1 dash agave nectar
Splash Parallel 49 Tricycle Grapefruit Radler

Place salt on a small plate. Cut a small wedge from lime. Squeeze out 4 tsp juice. Swipe wedge from halfway down one side of a glass up to the rim. Press into salt. Add watermelon slice to a small collins glass. Fill with ice. Pour in infused tequila, lime juice and agave nectar. Top with radler, stirring to mix.

Makes 1 drink

> *Watermelon and Campari–Infused Tequila* <

1 cup blanco tequila
¼ small watermelon,
    chopped (approximately 2 cups)
1 ½ oz Campari

1 ½ oz Aperol
2 Tbsp granulated sugar
4-cup jar with new lid and ring,
    sterilized

Remove seeds from watermelon, if needed. Place all ingredients in jar. Shake. Let stand for at least 24 hours. Pulse with a hand blender. Strain through a large sieve lined with several layers of cheesecloth into a large measuring cup or bowl. Use the bottom of a ladle to swirl and press any solids. Return to rinsed jar. Infused tequila will keep well, sealed and refrigerated, for at least 1 week. Makes 16 oz (2 cups), for 8 drinks

BOB & DOUG'S STRANGE BREW

When the McKenzie brothers, Canada's beer-loving hoseheads from the 1983 film *Strange Brew*, go to Elsinore Brewery to collect their well-deserved free case of beer, they were actually at the Old Fort Brewery in Prince George. The bizarre and addictive combination of flavours in this drink also celebrates the province's craft beer scene. Use your favourite stout for the syrup and your preferred lager to top it up.

1 ½ oz smoky mezcal
½ oz freshly squeezed lime juice
½ oz Rich Stout Syrup
2 dashes Bittered Sling Grapefruit and
   Hops bitters
2 to 3 rings fresh hot pepper, such as jalapeño
   (adjust amount depending on preferred
   heat intensity)
2 handfuls of ice cubes
3 to 4 oz chilled lager, such as Phillips Brewing
   Elsinore Lager

Pour all ingredients except ice and lager into a cocktail shaker. Add 1 large handful of ice. Shake until chilled. Double strain through a Hawthorne strainer and a fine-mesh strainer into a chilled fizz glass filled with remaining ice. Top with lager.

Makes 1 drink

> *Rich Stout Syrup* <

Pour 2 cups stout into a small saucepan. Stir to reduce carbonation. Bring beer to a boil over medium-high heat, stirring constantly. (If it bubbles up, briefly remove from heat.) Adjust heat so mixture is gently boiling. Cook until reduced to exactly 1 cup, 20 to 30 minutes. Reduce heat to medium. Add 2 cups demerara sugar and a generous pinch of salt, stirring often until dissolved. Remove from heat and let cool completely. Pour through a funnel lined with several layers of cheesecloth into a 2-cup sterilized jar. Syrup will keep, sealed and refrigerated, for 2 weeks or up to 1 month. Makes 16 oz (2 cups), for 32 drinks

SUNKEN PORT

KATIE MCDONALD gives painstaking consideration to each cocktail preparation detail, from the igniting of a cracked-black-pepper garnish to generously rubbing citrus on the exterior of the glass far below the rim, a technique that imparts flavour and scent on your fingertips as you sip away. In this cocktail, Katie plays around with the density of port-style fortified wine. Experimenting, she tried to float the wine on the surface of the drink but it sank to the bottom, hence the name.

2 oz Victoria Spirits Oaken Gin
¼ oz Honey Syrup (page 183)
2 dashes Bittered Sling Plum & Rootbeer
   bitters
Handful of ice cubes
1 large ice cube
¼ oz port-style fortified red wine, such as
   Gray Monk Odyssey III

Pour gin, honey syrup and bitters into a cocktail shaker or mixing glass. Add handful of ice cubes and stir until chilled. Strain through a julep strainer over large ice cube in an old-fashioned glass. Rest the back of a spoon over the surface of the drink without submerging it. Pour fortified wine slowly down the spoon; it should sink to the bottom of the drink.

Makes 1 drink

KATIE'S HONEY TIP

Use a local wildflower honey for this cocktail. She uses honey from a friend's hive.

WHAT'S UP, DOC?

Veteran SIMON OGDEN has been working in the industry for more than twenty years. He heads up the stellar bar program at Veneto Tapa Lounge in Victoria and oversees its dynamite cocktail list. This drink is a testament to his creativity. For this savoury cocktail inspired by Victoria's healthy lifestyle, Simon has incorporated garden-fresh ingredients. It's potent, so feel free to top with a touch more carrot juice.

2 oz Turmeric-Infused Rum
1 oz chilled freshly squeezed carrot juice
½ oz Honey Syrup (page 183)
3 dashes Bittered Sling Cascade Celery bitters
Handful of ice cubes
1 sprig fresh dill, for garnish

Pour all ingredients except ice and garnish into a mixing glass. Add ice. Stir well. Taste and add more carrot juice, if you like. Strain through a julep strainer into a cocktail glass. Smack dill a little to release the lovely aromatics, then garnish cocktail with it.

Makes 1 drink

> *Turmeric-Infused Rum* <

Pour 2 cups Mount Gay Eclipse Barbados Rum into a 2-cup sterilized jar. Add 2 tsp ground turmeric. Seal with a new lid and ring. Shake. Let stand for 2 minutes. Stir to incorporate ingredients, then strain through a coffee filter–lined funnel into another jar. Infused rum will keep at room temperature for months. Makes 16 oz (2 cups), for 8 drinks

THE EMPEROR

UVA Wine & Cocktail bar manager Lauren Mote is known for her bar skills and for her company Bittered Sling Extracts, which she co-owns with chef Jonathan Chovancek. Her cocktail is inspired by winemaker/farmer Masa Shiroki, who grows Ginpu rice in the Fraser Valley, which he uses to produce award-winning sake.

1 cucumber ribbon
1 oz Victoria Spirits Victoria Gin
1 oz Osake Fraser Valley Junmai Nigori Sake
¾ oz Pear-Infused Vermouth
½ oz Toasted Koshihikari Rice & Sesame Syrup
2 dashes Bittered Sling Cascade Celery bitters
Handful of ice cubes

Using a vegetable peeler, pull a long thin ribbon from cucumber. Chill a large coupe glass, then garnish interior with cucumber ribbon, cutting to fit, if needed. Add remaining ingredients except ice to a mixing glass. Add ice and stir gently until chilled. Strain through a julep strainer into the chilled and garnished coupe glass.
Makes 1 drink

> *Toasted Koshihikari Rice & Sesame Syrup* <

Pour ½ cup organic koshihikari rice into a skillet set over medium. Stir constantly, until golden, 5 to 7 minutes. Turn into a mortar and pestle. Place ¾ tsp sesame seeds in pan. Cook, stirring constantly, until golden brown, 1 to 3 minutes. Add to the mortar and pestle. Pound and grind as best you can. Bring ¾ cup + 2 Tbsp water to a boil in a small saucepan. Add 1 cup granulated sugar, stirring until dissolved. Remove from heat. Stir in rice mixture and 1/8 tsp kosher salt. Cover and let steep until cool. Add to a jar. Steep in the fridge for 48 hours. Fine strain through a coffee, wine or micro filter several times, until all particles are removed. Will keep, sealed and refrigerated, for up to 10 days. Makes 5 oz (2/3 cup), for 10 drinks

> *Pear-Infused Vermouth* <

Cut ½ semi-ripe Bartlett pears into chunks and place in 2-cup jar. Add 1 cup Cinzano dry white vermouth. Seal and refrigerate for 96 hours. Using a coffee, wine or micro filter, strain pear bits from vermouth into a 1-cup jar. Add 1 ½ tsp Okanagan Spirits Poire Williams Eau de Vie. Will keep well, sealed and refrigerated, for up to 10 days. Makes 8 oz (1 cup), for 10 drinks

SMOKY LAKE OLD-FASHIONED

DANIELLE TATARIN's fascination with all things liquid led her to start her own cocktail-centric company, West Coast Garnish Girls, and later, the Designer Cocktail Company. She runs the well-loved Keefer Bar in Vancouver's Chinatown, a bar which takes an apothecary-like approach to satiating spirituous cravings. Check out Danielle's wonderful take on the Old-Fashioned, with its nostalgic nod to flavours and aromas from Smoky Lake, near her childhood home in Alberta. This recipe calls for only a barspoon of her Smoked Spruce Syrup, but the subtle smokiness is worth the effort of making it.

2 oz Gibson's Finest 12 Year Old Canadian
   Whisky
1 barspoon Smoked Spruce Syrup
3 dashes Angostura bitters
Handful of ice cubes
1 large ice cube
1 lemon peel strip
2 brandied cherries, for garnish (optional)

Pour all ingredients except ice, lemon peel and cherries into a cocktail shaker. Add handful of ice cubes and stir until chilled. Strain through a julep strainer over large ice cube in a chilled highball glass. Pull a long strip of lemon peel over the glass, releasing oils into cocktail. Gently pinch, peel side out, misting oils over surface of the drink. Rub peel around the outside rim of the glass, then add. Garnish with a skewer of brandied cherries, if you like.
Makes 1 drink

> *Smoked Spruce Syrup* <

Bring 1 cup hot water to a boil in a small saucepan set over high heat. Reduce heat to medium. Add 2 cups granulated sugar and stir until dissolved. Pour syrup into a metal cocktail shaker base. Place 1 fresh spruce sprig, about 7 inches long and well rinsed, in syrup. Leave approximately 3 inches of sprig standing out of syrup. Wearing an oven mitt, place a mixing glass over sprig and, using a small kitchen blowtorch, ignite sprig until smoking (but without major flames). Carefully extinguish the flame with the mixing glass, capturing the smoke. Close shaker, using the mixing glass as the lid. Let stand for 10 minutes. Repeat this whole process three more times, finishing by closing shaker and allowing syrup to stand overnight. When ready, strain syrup through a fine-mesh strainer into a sterilized jar. Syrup will keep, sealed and refrigerated, for 2 weeks. Makes 14 oz (1 ¾ cups), for dozens of drinks

CAMPFIRE FLIP

ROBERT HOLL-ALLEN, affectionately referred to as "H," is known for the education nights he hosts on a regular basis at Notturno in Vancouver's Gastown, and for his imaginative cocktails—of which this drink is a fine example. Think of it as a sophisticated s'more in a glass!

1 oz Canadian whisky

1 oz French brandy

1 oz Maple Marshmallow Syrup

1 whole egg

Handful of ice cubes

Dark chocolate shavings, for garnish

1 small piece graham cracker, for garnish

Pour all ingredients except ice and garnishes into a cocktail shaker. Dry shake until incorporated and frothy. Add ice and shake until chilled. Double strain through a Hawthorne strainer and a fine-mesh strainer into a chilled small wine glass. Garnish with chocolate and graham cracker.

Makes 1 drink

> *Maple Marshmallow Syrup* <

Pour ½ cup maple syrup and ⅓ cup water in a small saucepan. Set over medium heat. Add 5 regular marshmallows. Bring mixture to a boil, stirring frequently until marshmallows dissolve, 8 to 10 minutes, and reducing heat if mixture is boiling too rapidly. Remove from heat and let cool completely. Strain through a sieve into a sterilized jar. Syrup will keep well, sealed and refrigerated, for 2 weeks. Makes 5 oz (⅔ cup), for 5 to 6 drinks

BUTCHART GARDEN SWIZZLE

Just outside Victoria, Vancouver Island's "City of Gardens," are the even more breath-taking Butchart Gardens. What began as a limestone quarry eventually blossomed into a diverse garden and worldwide attraction thanks to Robert Pim and Jennie Butchart. In the early 1900s, anyone who ventured to visit the gardens was offered free high tea, until it became too difficult to keep up with the throngs of visitors. Our Butchart Garden Swizzle pays homage to the gardens and to the tradition of high tea. Victoria Spirits Left Coast Hemp Vodka (distilled just around the corner from the gardens) is infused with Silk Road Tea's Seamist tea; the drink is then swirled with floral crème de violette and fresh mint leaves.

6 to 8 fresh mint leaves

¼ oz Rich Syrup (page 183)

Crushed ice

2 oz Seamist Tea–Infused Vodka (page 184)

1 oz crème de violette or violet liqueur

½ oz freshly squeezed lemon juice

1 to 2 dashes Bittered Sling Kensington
    Dry Aromatic bitters or Angostura bitters

2 to 3 oz chilled club soda

Place mint leaves in a collins glass. Add Rich Syrup. Muddle gently to release oils from mint. Fill the glass with ice. Add vodka, crème de violette, lemon juice and bitters to glass. Using a swizzle stick or barspoon, stir until chilled. Top with more ice. Stir in soda. Stir once more to incorporate. Serve with a straw.

Makes 1 drink

TEA TIP

The Seamist tea, made by Silk Road Tea in Victoria, is a compelling blend of mint and seaweed, but if you don't have access to it, your favourite mint tea will do the trick.

The
PRAIRIES

RECIPES IN THIS SECTION:

WHOOP-UP BUG JUICE

A BIT OF NORTHERN HOSPITALITY

CHINOOK SANGRIA

THE PEARL PUNCH

SPICED PEACH SPRITZ

BONITA APPLEBAUM

GINS & NEEDLES

THE STAMPEDER

THE LOOSE JAW

THE FLATLANDER'S FIZZ

DEVIL'S BARREL

SASKATOON BERRY & WHEAT BEER COCKTAIL

PRAIRIE CAESAR

LORD STANLEY'S PUNCH

FLINTABBATEY FLONATIN'S SUNLESS CITY SIPPER

GOLDEN BOY

Back on the hunt for the country's best cocktails, we continue eastward toward the Prairies. Our tiny rental car, heavy with the weight of our newly acquired bottles, proved faithful as we climbed into Alberta. The drive to Banff blew by with non-stop magnificent scenery amplified by a Canadian playlist. Roadside snacks at scenic lookouts broke up the long stretches, and the promise of enjoying an exquisite bottle of Blue Mountain Vineyards and Cellars Pinot Noir at our serene hotel room at the Banff Centre made the trip pleasant and relaxing. Quietly situated a short hike from downtown, the centre made for a great home base. Thanks to Banff National Park's *Performance in the Park,* we had the chance to hear some of the incredible Canadian artists we had listened to on the drive live in concert in an open yet intimate and absurdly picturesque concert setting. We were *sans* cocktails but filled with Canadian spirit. Banff is inspiring at every turn, and so we headed off to Calgary feeling fully charged.

Calgary was buzzing with energy, and upon arrival we instantly set out for drinks. On the advice of several bartenders in Vancouver and Victoria, we went to Model Milk for a fabulous dinner, which involved some of the best beef (Alberta beef, obviously) we've ever tasted and, of course, outstanding cocktails to kick off the evening. We even had the pleasure of sucking down a Model Milk Pimm's Cup in its one and only antique Pimm's-style glass, on loan from head bartender David Bain's home collection.

There are plenty of spots to choose from near 17th Street and 4th Avenue. Must-try spots are Milk Tiger Lounge (see co-owner Nathan Head's recipe, page 70) and happy hour at Añejo Restaurant—it's got a great tequila and mezcal selection. Then there's Raw Bar by Duncan Ly in Hotel Arts, where barman Dylan Cann shook up frothy drinks MacGyver style with the assistance of a spring from a Hawthorne strainer. We are pleased to feature a recipe from Raw Bar's general manager and mixologist Christina Mah (page 74).

We headed to Crowfoot Wine & Spirits and scanned the giant store for a good hour, picking up some western-made treasures like local mead and Three Point Vodka from Eau Claire Distillery, both used in our Chinook Sangria (page 71).

We didn't make it to Edmonton this time. However, we did get a taste of the growing scene there by way of testing Three Boars Eatery co-owner Chuck Elves' Gins & Needles recipe (page 77).

Farther east, as the land completely levels out, we came to the low-lying prairies, named after the French word for meadow. Much of the beautiful sprawling grassland of Saskatchewan and Manitoba was converted into crops, taking advantage of the region's long growing season. Wheat, barley and corn are just a few of the most widely sown grains in this region and are used worldwide in beer and spirit production.

It's no surprise that the Prairies were a major hot spot during Prohibition. Cities like Saskatoon, Moose Jaw and Bienfait played key roles in supplying our thirsty neighbours south of the border with illegal hooch. Notorious gangsters like Al Capone and Dutch Schultz are rumoured to have made appearances in seemingly quiet Prairie towns, meeting up with sordid characters like Diamond Jim Grady, who oversaw local bootlegging operations in Moose Jaw. Hotels like the Empress (which has since burnt down) made perfect base camps for travelling to and from nearby boozoriums, the booze-filled barns outside the cities. The creation of a network of underground tunnels provided a relatively safe place to store hooch, allowing hotel bars access to the illegal liquor and facilitating the smuggling of booze into the United States, all while offering an inconspicuous escape route. You can tour the tunnels and learn more about the Prairies' boozy

stamp on history at the Tunnels of Moose Jaw, a theatrical tour. Also, check out our Loose Jaw cocktail (page 81), which pays homage to Moose Jaw's spirituous past.

To enjoy local flavours and thirst-quenching cocktails today, there's no need to hide out in basement bars or risk hastily abandoning your drink to escape through the tunnels. In fact, the old Moose Jaw Canadian Pacific Railway Station, which was among the biggest centres of illegal alcohol distribution during Prohibition, has been converted into one of the most beautiful liquor stores in Canada.

Nowadays, beer is king in the Prairies, with breweries such as Great Western, Bin Brewing, Prairie Sun and Half Pints making a name for themselves. There are also local producers who brew for their own establishments, like Slow Pub and Bushwakker Brewpub in Regina. Bushwakker's annual limited-production blackberry mead release is revered by locals. It is in such high demand that on the first Saturday of December, devotees line up around the block, some waiting overnight in minus 40 degree weather for the doors to open and bottles of the exotic Lumsden Valley honey nectar infused with puréed blackberries to be released. Once open, the brewpub usually sells over 6,000 bottles within two hours. We would have loved to include the famed mead in a cocktail, but we couldn't get our hands on a bottle. Braving the line will have to remain on our cross-Canada cocktail bucket list for now.

Wine and spirits such as whisky and vodka are hugely popular in Saskatchewan and Manitoba as well. Crown Royal is a favourite and is produced on the western shore of Lake Winnipeg, in Gimli. This setting, with its natural local grains, pure water source and ideal climate to support the distilling process, contributes to Crown Royal's smooth blend. Available exclusively in Canada until 1964, Crown Royal is now the top-selling Canadian whisky in the United States. The Prairies are also home to smaller distilleries, which contribute a wide range of spirits and liqueurs. Standouts include Last Mountain, Lucky Bastards and Sperling. In fact, Sperling Distillery makes a tequila-esque spirit, more appropriately and legally permissibly named Saskatchewan cactus juice.

One of the best ways to get your hands on some liquid pride of the Prairies is to stop by a farmers' market. Aside from fantastic foraged goods and locally made specialties—like sea buckthorn berries, wild berry jams and fresh-baked loaves—at select markets you can also find regionally produced beer, wine and spirits. One stop at the Saskatoon Farmers' Market, for instance, will supply you with everything you'd need for our Saskatoon Berry & Wheat Beer Cocktail (page 84) and The Flatlander's Fizz (page 82).

We foresee cocktails becoming more prevalent in the Prairies, especially with restaurants and bars obtaining distilling licences and mixing up their own handcrafted goods. With so many flavours and fresh produce at hand, the possibilities for creative potations are endless. Enjoy some of our original cocktails and tales within the coming pages—each inspired by Alberta, Saskatchewan and Manitoba's vibrant culture, rich history and distinct agriculture.

WHOOP-UP BUG JUICE

The earliest incarnation of the Royal Canadian Mounted Police was formed in 1873, in part to help quell the chaos at trading posts such as Fort Whoop Up (now a historical site in Lethbridge). Bug juice—essentially flavoured hooch and one of the earliest "cocktails" invented on Canadian soil—was part of the problem. Early references describe it as a mixture of "alcohol spiked with ginger, molasses and red pepper, then coloured with black chewing tobacco, watered down and boiled to make firewater." We've taken some liberties and re-envisioned it as the ultimate Rum and Coke.

1 red bell pepper
½ oz Ginger Syrup (page 182)
2 oz dark rum, such as Havana Club Añejo
    7 Year Old Rum
½ oz freshly squeezed lemon juice
1 to 2 dashes Scrappy's Firewater bitters
    (optional)
1 dash Angostura bitters
Large handful of large ice cubes
Crushed ice
2 to 3 oz chilled cola
1 long lemon peel strip
1 piece candied ginger, for garnish

Cut a 1 ¼–inch thick slice of bell pepper. Place in a cocktail shaker along with ginger syrup and muddle. Add rum, lemon juice and bitters. Add handful of ice cubes. Shake until chilled. Double strain through a Hawthorne strainer and a fine-mesh strainer into a chilled old-fashioned glass filled with crushed ice. Stir in cola. Flame lemon peel (see page 6) over drink, rub the outside rim of the glass with flambéed peel, then discard peel. Garnish drink with candied ginger.

Makes 1 drink

BOTTLE BASICS

Dark rum is molasses derived, but it also showcases other flavours, such as citrus, nuts and even leather and tobacco. Since these flavour profiles parallel the original bug juice/firewater, we made it the base for our updated twist.

A BIT OF NORTHERN HOSPITALITY

Calgary-born NATHAN HEAD is co-owner of Milk Tiger Lounge. This truly Albertan cocktail features rye whisky made with local grains, and Old Style Pilsner, originally brewed in Lethbridge, where it's been made in the same style for almost a century. This tea-laced concoction balances the bold ingredients with sweet-bitter amaro and astringent black tea.

1 ½ oz Alberta Premium Dark Horse Rye
½ oz Amaro Averna
½ oz Black Tea Syrup
½ oz freshly squeezed lemon juice
2 handfuls of ice cubes
1 oz Pilsner Infusion

Pour all ingredients except ice and Pilsner Infusion into a cocktail shaker. Add 1 handful of ice. Shake until chilled. Double strain through a Hawthorne strainer and a fine-mesh strainer into a chilled beer glass filled with remaining ice. Top with Pilsner Infusion.
Makes 1 drink

> Black Tea Syrup <

Bring 1 cup water to a boil in a small saucepan. Add 1 cup granulated sugar, stirring until dissolved. Add 2 orange pekoe tea bags and let steep for 5 minutes. Remove and discard tea bags. Cool syrup. If making ahead, pour into a 2-cup sterilized jar with a new lid and ring. Syrup will keep, sealed and refrigerated, for 2 weeks.

> Pilsner Infusion <

Just before preparing cocktail, pour 1 room-temperature bottle (355 mL) Old Style Pilsner into a large measuring cup. Add 2 Earl Grey tea bags and let steep for 10 minutes. Remove and discard tea bags. Infusion will keep, refrigerated, for at least 1 hour. This recipe makes enough for a dozen cocktails, so whip up a batch when you're serving a crowd.

CHINOOK SANGRIA

Fortified with local vodka and sweetened with honey, this mead-based Sangria boasts a gorgeous, subtle-sweet off-dry flavour. The bee pollen rimmer is a wonderfully potent addition. Enjoy this recipe as a summertime sipper or bust it out when you get one of those lengthy Chinook temperature spikes. (See drink photo on page 33.)

1 Tbsp bee pollen
1 Tbsp granulated sugar
1 lemon
3 oz honey wine, such as Chinook Arch
    Meadery's King Arthur's Dry Mead
1 oz vodka, such as Eau Claire Distillery
    Three Point
½ oz Dry Curacao
½ oz Honey Syrup (page 183)
Handful of ice cubes
Crushed ice
1 oz chilled club soda

Pound bee pollen in a mortar and pestle until ground. Add sugar. Gently pound and mix to make rimmer. Place on a small plate. Cut a small wedge from lemon. Squeeze around rim of a wine glass. Turn the outside rim of the glass in rimmer. Squeeze and fine strain ½ oz juice from lemon through a fine-mesh strainer into a cocktail shaker. Add remaining ingredients except ice and soda. Add handful of ice cubes. Shake until chilled. Double strain through a Hawthorne strainer and a fine-mesh strainer into a chilled wine glass filled with crushed ice. Top with soda, stirring to mix.

Makes 1 drink

Dr. Scott's Completely Unfounded Headache Theory

Chinooks are said to be partly to blame for the number of migraines Albertans suffer, and there are also many who believe that honey will stave off migraines and other headaches. Couldn't hurt to give this a try, anyway!

BOTTLE BASICS

Honey wines and meads are an exciting and viable option for vintners in areas with less than ideal wine-growing conditions. It's no surprise that we are seeing more and more pop up across the country. Chinook Arch was the first honey winery in Alberta—a spinoff of the Chinook Honey Company.

THE PEARL PUNCH

Thirst-quenching barley water is basically a Wimbledon athlete's staple—refreshing, revitalizing and satiating in the heat. To create this punch, we combined our own homemade version with another sports-associated drink, an Arnold Palmer, a mix of iced tea and lemonade named for the golfer who made it famous. The result of the combination is a big-batch drink that's excellent on its own or with just a splash of your favourite spirit.

2 to 3 lemons or a mix of lemon and orange
⅓ cup granulated sugar
8 cups water
1 cup pearl barley, rinsed
3 orange pekoe tea bags
4 ½ oz shochu, gin, whisky or vodka (optional)
Handfuls of ice cubes

Pull 18 long, thick strips of peel from citrus. Add to a large pitcher along with sugar and muddle. Squeeze and fine strain ½ cup juice from lemons through a fine-mesh strainer into citrus-sugar mixture (called an oleo saccharum). Let stand for 30 to 60 minutes.

Meanwhile, place water and barley in a large saucepan. Bring to a boil over high heat. Reduce heat and simmer for 30 minutes. Fine strain into another pitcher or a bowl. Add tea bags and let steep for 6 minutes. Remove tea bags. Stir barley mixture into citrus-sugar mixture. Chill for at least 3 hours. Excellent served as is over ice, or mix each 5 oz serving with ½ oz of your favourite spirit.

Makes 8 to 10 drinks

BARLEY
Canada is one of the world's largest producers of barley, much of it coming out of Alberta. We used the leftover cooked and strained barley in a salad. Simply toss with vinaigrette and chopped fresh herbs, such as dill, or tarragon and chives.

SPICED PEACH SPRITZ

CHRISTINA MAH was born and raised in Calgary, where she got her start at Raw Bar by Duncan Ly, and she later returned to head up their bar program. This clean, crisp and light-tasting cocktail has layers of flavour thanks to the floral-and-fruity shrub plus bitters and spicy ginger beer.

1 ½ oz Hendrick's Gin
¼ oz Peach & Lavender Shrub
½ oz freshly squeezed lemon juice
2 dashes lavender bitters
2 large handfuls of ice cubes
3 oz chilled ginger beer
1 sprig fresh lavender, for garnish (optional)

Pour all ingredients except ice, ginger beer and garnish into a cocktail shaker. Add 1 handful of ice cubes. Shake vigorously until chilled. Double strain through a Hawthorne strainer and a fine-mesh strainer into a chilled collins glass. Top with more ice and ginger beer. Garnish with lavender sprig, if you like.
Makes 1 drink

> *Peach & Lavender Shrub* <

3 fresh peaches
½ lemon
1 ½ tsp dried lavender
1-inch cinnamon stick
4 black peppercorns

1 whole clove
1 ¼ cups granulated sugar
1 ¼ cups white wine vinegar
2-cup jar with new lid and ring, sterilized

Cut peaches into large slices and place in a resealable container. Using a rasp, zest lemon. Add to peaches along with lavender, cinnamon, peppercorns and clove. Add sugar. Cover and gently shake to coat fruit with sugar. Let stand at room temperature overnight. Pour vinegar over ingredients. Let stand at room temperature for another night. When ingredients are ready scrape into a medium saucepan. Bring to a boil over high heat. Reduce heat to medium. Simmer for 10 minutes. Remove from heat and let cool completely. Fine strain through a sieve, then a funnel lined with several layers of cheesecloth, into a jar. Syrup will keep, sealed and refrigerated, for at least 2 weeks. Makes 14 oz (1 ¾ cups), for a lot of drinks

BONITA APPLEBAUM

STEPHEN PHIPPS is a serious player on the Calgary cocktail scene, developing fantastic menus for Model Milk and the speakeasy-style Bourbon Room, located upstairs from the beer hall in National. Stephen favours savoury cocktails over sweet and has balanced the best of both in this autumn-friendly cocktail. He suggests smoking the chili flakes with applewood chips before making the syrup.

2oz Buffalo Trace Bourbon
1 ½ oz fresh pressed apple juice
¾ oz freshly squeezed lime juice
½ oz Chili Syrup
3 to 4 fresh sage leaves
Large handful of ice cubes

Pour all ingredients except ice into a cocktail shaker. Add ice and shake vigorously for 10 to 15 seconds. Double strain through a Hawthorne strainer and a fine-mesh strainer into a chilled coupe glass.

Makes 1 drink

> *Chili Syrup* <

Place 2 cups granulated sugar, 2 cups water and 1 ½ tsp chili flakes (preferably smoked) in a small saucepan. Set over medium-high heat. Bring to a boil, then reduce heat to medium. Cook until very syrupy, 12 to 15 minutes. Remove from heat and let cool completely. Fine strain to remove chili flakes. Store in a sterilized jar with a new lid and ring. Syrup will keep, sealed and refrigerated, for 2 weeks. Makes 20 oz (2 ½ cups), for 40 drinks

GINS & NEEDLES

Having moved from Red Deer to Edmonton, CHUCK ELVES is excited to be a part of a burgeoning cocktail scene in his adopted hometown. This primarily self-taught bar manager is co-owner of Three Boars Eatery. Here we feature his intensely woodsy Gins & Needles, which is spiked with homemade spruce liqueur. His toast to northern flavours seriously smacks of foresty aroma.

1 ½ oz Spirit Bear Gin
½ oz House Spruce Liqueur
¼ oz Dolin de Chambéry dry vermouth
4 drops Scrappy's Cardamom bitters
Small handful of ice cubes
¼ oz Fernet Branca
1 small spruce tip, for garnish (optional)

Pour all ingredients except ice, Fernet and garnish into a mixing glass. Add ice and stir until chilled. Strain through a julep strainer into a chilled coupe glass. Float Fernet overtop. Garnish with spruce tip, if you like.
Makes 1 drink

> *House Spruce Liqueur* <

Gather spruce branches. Chuck prefers older ones. You'll need approximately 30 inches to weigh ¾ oz (20 g) in total; this could be many small pieces. Thoroughly rinse. Remove needles and place in a sterilized 2-cup jar. Pour ⅔ cup high-proof (ideally 94%) neutral-grain spirit, such as Everclear or Global Alcool, overtop. Add ⅓ cup water. Seal and shake. Let stand at room temperature in a dark place until flavours infuse to your liking, 1 to 7 days. Fine strain through a funnel lined with several layers of cheesecloth into a small saucepan. Add ½ cup granulated sugar. Set over low heat. Cook, stirring, until sugar is dissolved. Remove from heat and let cool completely. Pour into a 2-cup sterilized jar. Liqueur will keep, sealed and stored in a cool, dark place, for at least 3 months. Makes 8 oz (1 cup), for 16 drinks

THE STAMPEDER

Also known as "Stampede City" and as "Cowtown," Calgary is definitely the cowboy capital of Alberta or, as some know it, the "Texas of the North." The city is also known for its annual stampede, which sells over a million tickets each year. Our Stampeder is a combination of a Bullshot—a savoury beef-broth drink—and the Caesar, Calgary's cocktail claim to fame. This drink celebrates true Albertan flavours and packs the restorative power to get you back in the saddle after a night on the town, stampede-style.

Large handful of ice cubes
1 ½ oz vodka, such as Eau Claire
    Distillery Three Point
3 to 6 dashes Worcestershire sauce
2 to 4 dashes hot sauce
1 small dollop horseradish (optional)
Generous grinding black pepper
4 ½ oz beef broth, preferably homemade
2 ½ to 3 oz chilled Tomato-Clam
    Juice (page 193) or store-bought
1 lemon wedge
1 celery stalk, for garnish
1 lemon wheel, for garnish (optional)
Pinch salt, for garnish (optional)

In an ice-filled highball or pint glass, build ingredients in the order listed, except lemon and garnishes. Squeeze in juice from lemon wedge, then drop wedge in drink. Stir to mix. Garnish with celery stalk and lemon wheel, if you like. Taste and stir in salt, if using, or more of the other seasonings, if you like.

Makes 1 drink

HOMEMADE VS. STORE-BOUGHT

If using a homemade beef broth or Tomato-Clam Juice, you may want to add extra salt and other seasonings. Feel free to play around with amounts. If using store-bought beef broth, check the package directions to see if it calls for dilution.

THE LOOSE JAW

During Prohibition days, Moose Jaw was often referred to as "Loose Jaw." A spin on the popular Canadian drink order Rye and Ginger seemed fitting for a cocktail of this name, as did that on a Prohibition classic like the Manhattan. We combined the two by lengthening with ginger ale. The result is a version of the Manhattan that goes down really easy. You may find yourself whipping up another round faster than usual.

2 oz Canadian whisky
½ oz dry vermouth
½ oz sweet red vermouth
2 dashes aromatic bitters
Handful of ice cubes
1 large ice cube
1 to 2 oz chilled ginger ale
1 homemade cocktail cherry (page 188)
    or store-bought, for garnish

Pour all ingredients except ginger ale and garnish into a mixing glass. Add handful of ice cubes and stir until chilled. Strain through a julep strainer over large ice cube into a chilled old-fashioned glass. Top with 1 oz ginger ale. Gently stir. Taste and add more, if you like. Skewer cherry and garnish cocktail.

Makes 1 drink

A Perfect Manhattan

This twist on a Perfect Manhattan—which calls for equal parts dry and sweet vermouth—can be made into the classic by simply omitting the ginger ale.

THE FLATLANDER'S FIZZ

This brightly hued, effervescent cocktail is thoroughly refreshing. Sea buckthorn is a berry that's cherished for its purported health benefits—it's high in vitamin C—but that didn't stop us from using it in a cocktail. (See drink photo on page 33.)

1 ½ oz gin
½ oz sea buckthorn liqueur, such as from LB Distillers or Okanagan Spirits
1 Tbsp sea buckthorn purée, such as from Northern Vigor Berries
½ oz freshly squeezed lemon juice
½ oz Simple Syrup (page 182)
Large handful of ice cubes
Crushed ice
1 oz chilled club soda, plus more to taste

Pour all ingredients except ice and soda into a cocktail shaker. Add ice cubes. Shake well until chilled. Fine strain into a chilled fizz glass filled with crushed ice. Top with 1 oz soda. Stir. Add more soda, if you like. Serve with a straw.
Makes 1 drink

Sea Buckthorn Berries

⊷⇒ ⇐⊶

These unusual golden- to crimson-coloured berries have an incredible and complex flavour—imagine sour and tangy citrus meets tropical fruits like pineapple and mango. Also known as sea berries, they grow well in poor and sandy soil. They're native to China but now grow in various parts of the world and, thanks to government incentives for farmers to grow them, more recently in Canada. We hope to see the berries become more widely available, but in the meantime, keep your eyes peeled for them.

DEVIL'S BARREL

São Paulo–born and Toronto-raised CHRISTOPHER CHO has worked all over Canada and has a passion for this country's homegrown ingredients. He gained plenty of notoriety at Calgary's successful Charcut restaurant but has recently taken up residency farther inland to head up the bar at the locally focused Ayden Kitchen and Bar in Saskatoon. Boasting perfectly-crafted classics and showcasing original concoctions, the drinks are part of what made this restaurant one of the top 10 contenders in enRoute's "Canada's Best New Restaurants 2014."

1 oz Forty Creek Barrel Select Whisky
¾ oz Aperol
½ oz calvados
¼ oz Honey Syrup (page 183)
¼ oz freshly squeezed lemon juice
2 dashes grapefruit bitters
2 handfuls of ice cubes
1 grapefruit peel strip

Pour all ingredients except ice and grapefruit peel into a cocktail shaker. Add 1 large handful of ice cubes and shake. Double strain through a Hawthorne strainer and a fine-mesh strainer into an old-fashioned glass filled with remaining ice. Pull a long strip of grapefruit peel over the glass, releasing oils into cocktail. Gently pinch, peel side out, misting oils over surface of the drink. Rub peel around the outside rim of the glass, then add.

Makes 1 drink

SASKATOON BERRY & WHEAT BEER COCKTAIL

Saskatchewan is known for its sprawling wheat fields, with their sunny glow. This is the inspiration for this refreshing Shandy-meets-Monaco cocktail that uses Saskatchewan liqueur and wheat beer. Whip up a recipe to serve two, or multiply for company.

2 oz Saskatoon berry liqueur, such as from LB Distillers

1 oz freshly squeezed lemon juice

12 oz chilled wheat beer, such as Prairie Sun 306 Urban Wheat Beer or 341 mL bottle of your favourite wheat beer

Divide liqueur between 2 chilled beer glasses. Add half of lemon juice to each glass. Slowly top each with beer.

Makes 2 drinks

BOTTLE BASICS

Can't get a hold of the Saskatchewan brands? Simply whip up this drink with local offerings. We had great results with other Saskatoon berry liqueurs, including Ironworks Distillery's, and Cidrerie et Vergers Pedneault's Crème de Petites Poire. This applies to wheat beers too. This beer cocktail also pairs well with Mill St. Belgian Wit or Half Pints Weizen Heimer.

PRAIRIE CAESAR

This flavourful spin on a Caesar highlights the agricultural pride of the Prairies. The toasted flaxseed rimmer is a perfect complement to the butter-washed grain-flavoured spirit. If you can't get your hands on unaged whisky, white dog or moonshine, a good grain-based vodka such as Still Waters Single Malt Vodka works as well.

Toasted Flaxseed Rimmer

1 lemon wedge

Large handful of ice cubes

1 ½ oz Brown Butter–Infused Unaged Whisky (page 185)

2 dashes hot sauce

1 dash Worcestershire sauce

Generous grinding black pepper

4 to 6 oz homemade Tomato-Clam Juice (page 193) or store-bought

Place rimmer on a small plate. Moisten the rim of a large highball or pint glass with lemon wedge. Turn the outside rim of the glass in rimmer. Fill glass with ice. Pour in whisky. Add hot sauce and Worcestershire. Sprinkle with pepper and squeeze in juice from lemon wedge. Top with Tomato-Clam Juice. Stir to mix and chill drink. Taste and adjust seasonings to your liking. Tasty served with sweet and salty popcorn.

Makes 1 drink

> Toasted Flaxseed Rimmer <

Place 2 Tbsp flaxseed in a small skillet set over medium heat. Heat seeds, stirring constantly, until aromatic and beginning to crackle, 5 to 7 minutes. Remove from heat and let cool completely. Grind in a spice or coffee grinder or pound with a mortar and pestle. Stir with 1 Tbsp celery salt and 1 tsp chili powder in a small bowl. Rimmer will keep in an airtight container for up to 1 month.

LORD STANLEY'S PUNCH

Canada owes one of its most famous hockey traditions to the 1896 Winnipeg Victorias hockey team, which was the first to drink champagne from Lord Stanley's Cup. This cocktail seemed appropriate given that the original trophy was a silver punch bowl. We've created an elegant, celebratory punch to serve for any special occasion that involves a large group—make a batch for the night of a big game.

3 to 6 regular or Meyer lemons
1 orange
½ cup maple sugar
8 oz Canadian whisky, preferably Crown Royal
4 oz maple syrup
6 to 8 dashes Angostura bitters
1 bottle (750 mL) chilled dry sparkling wine
2 cups chilled club soda
Ice ring (see below)

Pull long strips from 2 lemons and ½ of an orange, removing any white pith. Place in a punch bowl. Create an oleo saccharum by muddling citrus strips with maple sugar, releasing oil from peels, until a paste forms. Add half the whisky and lightly muddle. Cover and let stand at room temperature for 1 hour. Squeeze 6 oz juice from lemons. Add to punch mixture along with maple syrup, bitters and remaining whisky. Cover and let chill in fridge for 4 hours. Remove from fridge and add sparkling wine and soda. Stir lightly. Add prepared ice ring just before serving.
Makes 10 to 15 punch-sized drinks

> *Ice Ring* <

Prepare an ice ring by partially filling a Bundt pan (no larger than your punch bowl) with water. Thinly slice 1 lemon and ½ orange. Carefully arrange slices in bowl to overlap each other. Freeze ring overnight, at least 12 hours.

FLINTABBATEY FLONATIN'S SUNLESS CITY SIPPER

This refreshing Moscow Mule variation is dedicated to Manitoba mining town Flin Flon, the only Canadian city named after a science fiction character. The metal cup is inspired by the strange underground world filled with precious metals that Flintabbatey Flonatin stumbles upon, and the Riga Black Balsam reflects the hues of the sunless city.

1 ½ oz vodka
¾ oz freshly squeezed lemon juice
½ oz Riga Black Balsam liqueur
½ oz Simple Syrup (page 182)
Large handful of ice cubes
Crushed ice
1 oz chilled ginger beer

Pour all ingredients except ice and ginger beer into a cocktail shaker. Add ice cubes. Shake well until chilled. Strain through a Hawthorne strainer into a chilled mule or tin cup filled with crushed ice. Top up with ginger beer.
Makes 1 drink

BOTTLE BASICS

Riga Black Balsam is an extremely complex, bitter-sweet herbal liqueur from Latvia. It's made with twenty-four ingredients, including birch buds, raspberry and valerian root and some other top-secret ones. It is an acquired taste, but one well worth discovering. Enjoy over ice cream, straight up or mixed in cocktails.

GOLDEN BOY

This brightly hued statuesque cocktail is inspired by the famous wheat-sheaf bearing Golden Boy sculpture that overlooks Winnipeg from the Manitoba Legislative Building. The complex flavours of this drink are almost as intriguing as this building's architectural mysteries, secrets and symbols that are hidden in plain view—you can even take a tour on the topic.

2 oz aged aquavit, such as Aalborg Jubilaeums Akvavit
¾ oz Bärenjäger Honey Liqueur
½ oz freshly squeezed lemon juice
¼ oz Strega liqueur
¼ oz Simple Syrup (page 182)
⅛ tsp Three Farmers Camelina Oil or good-quality olive oil
Tiny pinch coarse kosher salt or fleur de sel
Large handful of ice cubes

Pour all ingredients except ice into a cocktail shaker. Add ice. Shake until chilled. Double strain through a Hawthorne strainer and a fine-mesh strainer into a chilled coupe glass.
Makes 1 drink

CAMELINA AND OLIVE OIL

Prairie-made Three Farmers Camelina Oil is created by cold-pressing camelina sativa oilseed. The result is an oil that carries a lovely, subtle nut flavour. It's essential for this cocktail that the oil, whether camelina or olive, is good quality. Otherwise, its flavour may overwhelm the drink, rather than contributing an interesting mouth-feel. If you don't have any in your cupboard, simply skip this addition.

The
MIDDLE

RECIPES IN THIS SECTION:

PIMM'S SPIN

BALSAM BLEND

MAN ABOUT CHINATOWN

PTB

SPADINA SPLASH

THE TORONTONIAN

RONALD CLAYTON

THE GARDINER

PEARY PUNCH

NORTH OF 44

CELERY RICKEY

THE CANADIAN R&R

PRINCE EDWARD BOUNTY

CANADIAN RYE DIRTY MARTINI

THE ALCHEMIST

CARIBOU

THE POLAR VORTEX

SAISON ROYALE

THE BOREAL COTTON-CANDY COCKTAIL

SWEET FERN G&T

SAUCIER'S SEIGNIORY SPECIAL

BLACK BEAUX-ARTS FIZZ

LA POMME DU DIABLE

We are no strangers to the regions in this upcoming chapter. Having spent most of our lives in Ontario, we are proud to call it home. And collectively, we've covered a lot of ground here—from Moosonee to Niagara, North Bay to Thunder Bay, and we have lived all over Canada's largest city, Toronto, where we are exposed to an overwhelming amount of diverse and delicious food and drink options. Scott also lived in Montreal for years and we often head to Quebec for weekend trips. It's not just sentimentality or the short drive that lead us in that direction with such frequency. Our main focus when travelling is delectable eats and libations, and la belle province has no shortage of indulgence opportunities. We believe strongly in creating good travel karma and repaying the favour of excellent recommendations. To honour that debt, here is our best advice for a Central Canada tippling trip.

In Toronto, we make regular stops at Kensington and St. Lawrence Markets, as well as hitting the farmers' markets to get the prime seasonal and harder-to-come-by locally produced and foraged goods. At St. Lawrence Market, we bounce around from vendor to vendor gathering the best produce, stocking up on exotic spices and, treating ourselves to fresh flowers. We satisfy our French, Spanish and, of course, Canadian cheese addictions at Scheffler's Delicatessen and scarf down a peameal bacon sandwich from Carousel Bakery. In Kensington Market and neighbouring Chinatown, we load up on ingredients from all over the world—South America, Mexico, the Caribbean, Asia, Europe—and locally made goods too. If the red light is on, we might pop into Cold Tea (named after a less-than-legal late-night Chinatown tradition), which is tucked away down a tiny hallway in the market. That's where we were first introduced to the drink stylings of Sarah Parniak (check out her PTB, page 103). These days, you can find her around the corner at People's Eatery.

When cocktail hour strikes, there's no lack of places to get a great drink in Toronto. The cocktail scene has been growing for years, steadily gaining momentum. We have celebrated many occasions over drinks at Hoof Cocktail Bar, where owner Jen Agg has coached us on proper techniques, though it's hard to say how much we remember, as we were sampling Hoof cocktails during the lesson (check out Celery Rickey, page 113). We adore creations at local haunt Geraldine in our neighbourhood of Parkdale, manned by Michael Mooney (check out his recipe dedicated to the area on page 108). We are also huge fans of the menus at Bar Isabel and the ambitious Bar Raval, with their all-star bar team including Robin Goodfellow (see his recipe, page 106). Just a few steps away you can enjoy intriguing cocktails and snacks at LoPan, which is upstairs from DaiLo, a must-try for dinner. There are far too many places for exceptional drinks to be able to name them all, but other stellar stomping grounds include The Harbord Room (see Dave Mitton's recipe, page 107), Bar Buca, Northwood and of course The Drake Hotel. We haven't even touched on beer and the amazing options like the innovative Bellwoods Brewery, Junction Craft Brewing, the east end Left Field Brewery or the distillery district gem Mill St., where they've actually started distilling. There, you'll also find Ontario Spring Water Sake Company where you can buy delicious, unpasteurized sake right from the source.

When we have a bit more time we venture out of the city to Ontario's wine regions, first swinging by Victoria's parents in the greenbelt, where meals are often made from the produce of their lush backyard. From there it's easy for us to extend these Hamilton family visits by heading farther south into Niagara wine country. In the Escarpment area, we hit favourites like Tawse Winery, and then Dillon's distillery in Beamsville, which is used often by Ontario mixologists. Dillon's uses Niagara grapes and other responsibly sourced fruits to make a wide range of spirits and bitters, some of which are only available on site. This cold-climate growing area, with its moist soil and elevated slopes, can support a huge diversity of crops such as peaches, apples and many varieties of grapes. Head farther south through the sub-appellations of the Niagara Peninsula toward the fertile, sandy soils of Niagara-on-the-Lake, or to the warmer Lake Erie North Shore to try out more seasonal releases and wines. Time your visit with new-release parties to enjoy music and dinner with your wine. One of the most anticipated events is the annual Icewine Festival, held in January. With over thirty wineries participating, you can revisit favourites and sample the new contenders.

Another gastronomically interesting region worth travelling to is Prince Edward County. We often head there to celebrate Victoria's birthday, which frequently falls on the weekend of Picton's annual Great Canadian Cheese Festival. What could be better than spending a weekend gorging and stocking up on Canadian cheese and wine? (See some of our favourites, page 197.) For an ideal county experience head to Norman Hardie Winery and Vineyard for exceptional wines and wood fired oven pizza or slot in a picnic at The Grange of Prince Edward Vineyard and Estate Winery. The region also has a superb selection of locally brewed beer and cider. We recommend visiting Barley Days Brewery in Picton and the County Cider Company in Waupoos. Ontario's craft beer boom is still resounding, and craft distilleries are on the rise across the province, making it an exciting time for locavore cocktail lovers.

If you're looking to get out of the city, go cottaging in the Kawarthas, Muskoka or Bruce Peninsula, or venture north to Scott's beautiful hometown of North Bay. No matter where you end up, our advice is to seek out local markets and to take your time and stop at fruit stands. Our Balsam Blend (page 101) celebrates ingredients that are on hand near the cottage. Pair these finds with purchases from onsite retail stores at wineries, breweries or distilleries (like Still Waters Distillery) on your way out of town.

Travelling eastward, we reach Quebec. Well known for its world-class beers and incredible craft breweries, it has also been an important player in promoting spirit culture in Canada. The province was home to the first Canadian tavern in 1648, the first commercial brewery in 1668 and the first distillery in 1769. The Québécois have been innovators in alcoholic production and also defenders of the right to drink: in an 1898 referendum, the high percentage of Quebec voters against Prohibition were essentially responsible for a federal bill on the ban not being introduced in Parliament. It was the only province to never go completely dry. Celebrated ice cider and apple brandy producer Domaine Pinnacle touts its location as being a lookout during rum-running days (you can try the company's tasty ice cider in our Pomme du Diable, page 130). Quebec cider is a prime example of a Canadian product that embodies terroir. Quebec distillers are constantly pushing booze boundaries and creating unique products, such as parsnip gin Piger Henricus from micro-distillery Les Distillateurs Subversifs (featured in The Alchemist, page 119). Domaine Pinnacle's Ungava gin exemplifies northern terroir with its blend of aromatics from northern Quebec. Companies dedicated to Québécois food culture like Société-Original and d'Origina Être Boréal are exploring flavours native to their turf, highlighting the benefits of harvesting close to home. We explore how these flavours transform classic cocktails, as in our Sweet Fern G&T (page 126).

In Quebec we love to see which flavours are filling cups and plates in the lively cities. In Montreal, small plates and cocktails at Hotel Herman (their Saison Royale is featured on page 122), beers and elevated pub grub at Maison Publique and truly incredible Caesars with seafood at Joe Beef are all just a taste of what this vibrant city has to offer. We suggest booking an unforgettable feast at the insanely indulgent Cabane à Sucre Au Pied de Cochon, situated not too far outside of the city. There are also countless places to simply enjoy a great drink, like the impressive cocktail bar Le Lab, traditional and Canadian-inspired sips at Dominion Square Tavern or finely executed classics at The Emerald. And we'd be remiss not to include the experience of sampling tasty brews at Dieu du Ciel.

Before leaving town, we take time to hit the markets. Atwater and Jean Talon Markets are amazing places to pick up produce, artisanal meats and cheeses, wild mushrooms and some of the best provincially made liqueurs, wines, beers, ciders, spirits, meads and hydromiels. Head to Les Douceurs du Marché in Atwater Market for bitters and other delicacies, and if you're at Jean Talon Market, browse Le Marché des Saveurs du Québec. They have an expansive collection of Québécois alcohols and other treats.

If you're in Quebec City, Marché du Vieux-Port is equally as impressive. Check out an extensive selection of herbs, spices and produce, then try various maple liqueurs and go by Cassis Monna & Filles for samples. Squeeze in a Canadian themed tipple at nearby Château Frontenac.

One-stop shopping at the markets is a great way to taste your way through the province but, if you have time, also take a trip to the agricultural areas surrounding the major cities. A drive along the St. Lawrence River to Charlevoix makes for an exceptional Canadian food and drink vacation. Once there, either Baie-Saint-Paul or La Malbaie will make an excellent home base for exploring the flavours of this rich region. Mesmerized by the arresting scenery, we explored leisurely, stopping at places such as La Ferme Basque for foie gras tastings or the innovative Domaine de la Vallée du Bras, which produces Omerto, their tomato-based aperitif wines. Stop for a market raid at Les Jardins du Centre before or after taking the ferry over to L'Isle-aux-Coudres. During the short drive around the island, you can grab traditional sugar pie and try out a plethora of ciders, liqueurs and mistelles at La Cidrerie et Vergers Pedneault. In the evening, try out one of Charlevoix's proudly local-focused restaurants. If you must prioritize, shop at the Cheese Economuseum in Baie-Saint-Paul. You can get your hands on most of the region's great selections right there.

In an attempt to attain more good "travel karma," we go beyond sharing trip tips and suggestions: within these pages you'll also find a travel guide by way of drinks created by both us and bar pros.

PIMM'S SPIN

When Ontario's strawberry season is flourishing, try mashing those ripe, succulent berries into this refreshing cocktail. Although you may use whichever berry is tastiest and available, we love the combo of sweet-tart strawberry and traditional borage in this Pimm's riff. Tiny pinches of salt and pepper act as enhancers, emphasizing the fresh flavours.

1 large or 3 small strawberries, sliced

4 tender baby borage leaves or 3 thin slices of cucumber, preferably seedless

2 oz Pimm's No. 1

2 tsp freshly squeezed lime juice

Tiny pinch each Maldon salt and freshly ground black pepper

Handful of ice cubes

4 to 4 ½ oz chilled ginger ale, plus more to taste

1 borage flower, for garnish (optional)

Place strawberries and borage into a chilled collins glass. Pour in Pimm's. Using a muddler or the handle of a wooden spoon, gently smash. Stir in lime juice, salt and pepper. Add ice cubes. Slowly top with ginger ale. Stir again. Add more ginger ale, if you like. Garnish with a borage flower, if you like.

Makes 1 drink

Borage

If you don't have borage leaves, use cucumber instead, and a strawberry or cucumber slice works well as a garnish in place of the borage flower. If using borage leaves, the tender baby ones are preferred, as they're less prickly than mature leaves. You can use mature ones if you like, but proceed at your own risk—we do. For more ideas on how to use borage, check out A Drinkable Garden (page 198).

BALSAM BLEND

This cottage-friendly cocktail is dedicated to Balsam Lake, Scott's family's summer sanctuary, but you can make it wherever you go for a rustic summer vacation. All you'll need is a handful of berries from a hike (or from a trip to a nearby fruit stand), plus a couple of standard bar bottles—Canadian whisky, vermouth, Angostura bitters—which maybe you have tucked away in a dusty cabin cupboard. Build a campfire, and if you're feeling adventurous, smoke the glass; otherwise, just enjoy this cocktail while watching the flames.

2 oz Pine-Infused Canadian Whisky (page 185)
1 scant oz sweet white or red vermouth or
    a combo of sweet and dry
1 dash Angostura bitters
Handful of ice cubes
1 large ice cube or 2 regular ice cubes
1 to 2 pieces Whisky-Soaked Wild Fruit
1 or 2 long pine needles (optional)

Smoke any cottage cocktail glass you have on hand (optional). Pour whisky, vermouth and bitters into a mixing glass. Add handful of ice cubes and stir until chilled. Strain through a julep strainer over 1 large ice cube in prepared glass. Serve garnished with soaked fruit skewered on pine needle, if you like.
Makes 1 drink

> *Whisky-Soaked Wild Fruit* <

Pour ¼ cup wild blueberries, raspberries, blackberries or strawberries in a small bowl. Using a fork, poke holes all over. Pour 1 Tbsp Canadian whisky overtop. Let stand for 30 minutes.

Campfire Smoked Glass

Carefully hold a sturdy heatproof glass near campfire smoke but away from the fire. Using a saucer, cover and capture the smoke in the glass. Set on the counter while you prepare the cocktail. Or, to prepare at home, place dried cedar bows over tin foil set on an unlit barbecue rack (propane turned off!). Using a barbecue lighter, ignite until smoking (but without major flames). Carefully place the glass overtop the smoke and small flame, if there is one. The glass should put out the fire immediately and smoke the inside of the glass. If it doesn't, carefully remove the glass. Extinguish fire.

MAN ABOUT CHINATOWN

ROBIN KAUFMAN is known in Toronto for his expertly crafted cocktails, which he serves at the members-only speakeasy style bar the Toronto Temperance Society. Members, or those lucky enough to be friends with one, can sample a wild assortment of hard to find spirits and liqueurs and enjoy delicious pre-prohibition style cocktails in a refined setting. Originally from Vancouver, Robin is inspired by the abundance of ingredients found in the vibrant Chinatowns of both Vancouver and Toronto. We love the savoury-sweet-sour flavour and black hue of the sesame syrup and how it softens into a beautiful frothy drink that intensifies as you enjoy it.

2 oz Lot No. 40 Canadian Whisky

1 oz Black Sesame Syrup

¾ oz freshly squeezed lemon juice

¾ oz or 1 small egg white

Handful of ice cubes

1 mandarin orange peel strip

Tiny pinch Chinese five-spice powder

Pour all ingredients except ice, orange peel and five-spice powder into a cocktail shaker. Shake until incorporated and frothy. Add ice and shake until chilled. Double strain through a Hawthorne strainer and a fine-mesh strainer into a chilled coupe glass, preferably crystal. Pull a strip of peel from orange. Gently pinch, peel side out, misting oils over frothy surface of the drink. Discard peel. Very lightly sprinkle five-spice powder overtop.

Makes 1 drink

>. Black Sesame Syrup <

1 cup black sesame seeds

1 cup water

½ cup white wine

½ cup honey

½ cup granulated sugar

2-cup jar with new lid and
ring, sterilized

Place sesame seeds in a small skillet. Set over medium heat. Cook until lightly toasted, about 5 minutes. Add water and wine to pan. Reduce slightly, about 5 minutes. Strain through a sieve into a measuring cup. Measure out 1 cup exactly of sesame liquid and pour into a saucepan. Add honey and sugar to sesame liquid. Set over medium heat. Stir occasionally until honey and sugar are dissolved. Let cool. Fine strain through a funnel lined with several layers of cheesecloth into jar. Syrup will keep, sealed and refrigerated, for at least 2 weeks. Makes 14 oz (1 ¾ cups), for 14 drinks

PTB

SARAH PARNIAK prides herself on whipping up custom-tailored libations and thrives on the spontaneity of requests. In fact, Sarah's PTB cocktail came to fruition thanks to the helping hand of a regular, and bares a namesake that is a mix of their names in abbreviation. It's also a nod to PT Barnum. When Sarah is not behind the stick, she regularly contributes to the local newspaper *NOW*, providing advice on where to get the best drinks, what must-have bottles are available in the LCBO and some of her own creative cocktail recipes.

1 ½ oz blended Scotch, such as Black Grouse
¾ oz amontillado sherry
¼ oz apricot liqueur, such as Luxardo
¼ oz amaro
1 dash orange bitters
Handful of ice cubes
1 ribbon peeled fresh ginger, for garnish

Pour all ingredients except ice and garnish in a mixing glass. Add ice and stir until chilled and slightly diluted, about 20 seconds. Strain through a julep strainer into a chilled coupe glass. Using a peeler, pull a ribbon of ginger and garnish drink with it.
Makes 1 drink

SPADINA SPLASH

This cocktail celebrates the vast array of flavours and ingredients found in Toronto's Chinatown. A quick trip to Spadina Avenue and you can pick up a plethora of exotic ingredients with cocktail-friendly flavour profiles, both sweet and savoury.

1 ½ oz gin
1 oz freshly squeezed grapefruit juice
1 oz chilled Junmai Nigori sake, such as
    Ontario Spring Water Sake Company
¾ oz Ginseng & Red Date Syrup
¼ oz Campari
2 dashes Bar 40 Umami bitters (optional)
Large handful of ice
Crushed ice
1 to 2 oz chilled club soda (optional)
1 red date, for garnish (optional)
1 triangular piece grapefruit wheel,
    for garnish (optional)

Pour all ingredients except ice, soda and garnishes into a cocktail shaker. Add ice cubes. Shake until chilled. Double strain through a Hawthorne strainer and a fine-mesh strainer into an ice-filled fizz or small collins glass. Top with a splash of soda. Garnish with a red date and grapefruit, if you like. This cocktail is especially satisfying served with noodles.
Makes 1 drink

> Ginseng & Red Date Syrup <

Dried red dates (also called jujubes) and fresh ginseng can be found in many Asian food stores. If unavailable, regular dried dates and dried ginseng may be substituted.

Rinse 1 cup dried red dates, pitted, and 3 pieces fresh ginseng, each 3 to 4 inches long. Cut ginseng into ¼-inch slices. Place 3 cups water, dates and ginseng in a saucepan. Set over medium-high heat. Bring to a boil, stirring occasionally. Let boil until liquid is flavourful and reduced by about two-thirds or to 1 cup but no less. This will take 20 to 30 minutes. Remove from heat and let cool slightly. Strain through a fine-mesh strainer into a measuring cup with a spout. Using the back of a spoon, lightly press solids to extract all liquid, noting the amount of liquid released. Pour liquid into rinsed saucepan. Add 1 to 1 ½ cups granulated sugar in an amount equal to liquid. Set saucepan over medium and heat mixture just until sugar is dissolved. Remove from heat and let cool completely. Fine strain through a funnel lined with several layers of cheesecloth into a sterilized jar. Syrup will keep, sealed and refrigerated, for at least 2 weeks. Makes 12 oz (1 ½ cups), for 18 drinks

THE TORONTONIAN

For years ROBIN GOODFELLOW pushed boundaries with his inventive Canadian-inspired cocktails as bar manager at URSA. He now co-owns Bar Raval, which is home to some of Toronto's culinary and bar megastars. This is his re-imagined version of the classic cocktail, The Toronto, which he chose to show his pride in being born and raised in Hogtown. His version includes St-Germain in place of simple syrup. It's a drink for Fernet Branca lovers but is also sure to convert those still wary of this delightfully bitter liqueur.

2 oz Lot No. 40 Canadian Whisky
2 tsp St-Germain Elderflower Liqueur
1 ½ tsp Fernet Branca
3 dashes Angostura bitters
Handful of ice cubes
1 orange peel strip

Pour all ingredients except ice and orange peel into a mixing glass. Add ice and stir until chilled. Strain through a julep strainer into a chilled coupe glass. Pull a long strip of orange peel over the glass, releasing oils into cocktail. Gently pinch, peel side out, misting oils over surface of the drink. Rub peel around the outside rim of the glass, then add.
Makes 1 drink

RONALD CLAYTON

DAVE MITTON worked at bars all over the world before setting up shop in Toronto. He's co-owner of the Harbord Room and THR and Co. This unique yet essentially classic cocktail is dedicated to Dave's grandfather, Ronald Clayton Mitton. The aromas captured in this cocktail are vivid reminders to Dave of the much loved man; they create a strong drink that is at the same time sweet, soft and gentle.

2 ½ oz Vanilla-Infused Lot
    No. 40 Canadian Whisky
½ oz Tobacco Syrup
2 dashes Urban Moonshine Organic Maple
    Digestive Bitters
Handful of ice cubes
1 large ice cube

Pour all ingredients except ice into a mixing glass. Add handful of ice cubes. Stir about 18 to 20 times to chill and blend mixture, being careful not to dilute the drink too much. Strain through a julep strainer over large ice cube in an old-fashioned glass.
Makes 1 drink

> Vanilla-Infused Lot No. 40 Canadian Whisky <

Split half a vanilla bean lengthwise with a paring knife. Use the blunt side of the knife to scrape out seeds. Place seeds and pod in a resealable jar containing 1 ½ cups whisky. Put on the lid and give the jar a shake. Let stand until flavour infuses, about 1 day. Remove vanilla. Strain liquid into a sterilized jar and seal with a new lid and ring. Infused whisky will keep, sealed and stored in a cool, dark place, for at least 3 months. This recipe is easily doubled. Makes 12 oz (1 ½ cups), for 5 drinks

> Tobacco Syrup <

Place 1 ½ cups Havana Club Añejo 7 Year Old Rum and 1 cup raw sugar, such as turbinado, in a saucepan. Set over medium heat. Bring to a simmer, stirring until sugar is dissolved. If alcohol ignites, place saucepan lid over flame to extinguish. Reduce heat to medium-low. Continue simmering until mixture is syrupy, 10 to 20 minutes. Carefully pour syrup through a sieve packed with 2 scoops Original Blend Amphora Pipe Tobacco into another saucepan. Repeat about 3 to 5 times, until you can smell tobacco in syrup. Strain well, removing all tobacco from syrup. Let cool, then transfer to a sterilized jar. Syrup will keep, sealed and refrigerated, for 2 weeks. Makes 10 oz (1 ¼ cups), for 20 drinks

THE GARDINER

MICHAEL MOONEY named this drink after the lakeside highway that played a major part in shaping Toronto's Parkdale neighbourhood. Construction of the Gardiner Expressway led to the demolition of the Sunnyside Amusement Park, changing the area dramatically from the thriving lakefront entertainment retreat it once was. Nowadays, places like Geraldine, with their fantastically complex drinks and equally stellar food menu, are bringing people from all over Toronto to enjoy one of the most thriving, eclectic, playful and diverse stretches of Toronto's west end.

2 pieces fresh rosemary, each 1 inch long
1 ¾ oz Alberta Premium Dark Horse Rye
½ oz green Chartreuse
½ oz Carpano Antica Formula or Cinzano
   sweet red vermouth
½ barspoon Fig Syrup
4 dashes Dillon's Small Batch Distillers
   Wormwood bitters
Handful of ice cubes
1 large ice cube

Muddle 1 piece of rosemary into a mixing glass. Add remaining ingredients except ice and rosemary. Add handful of ice cubes and stir until chilled, 20 to 30 seconds. Strain through a julep strainer over large ice cube in a double old-fashioned glass. Garnish with remaining rosemary sprig.

Makes 1 drink

> *Fig Syrup* <

Place 1 cup granulated sugar, 1 cup water and 8 dried figs in a small saucepan. Slowly heat over medium-low until figs soften. Gently break open figs with a wooden spoon to release their flavour. Cook for 5 minutes, being careful not to let mixture boil. Strain through a funnel lined with several layers of cheesecloth into a sterilized 2-cup jar. Seal with a new lid and ring. Syrup will keep, sealed and refrigerated, for at least 2 weeks. Makes 10 oz (1 ¼ cups), for a lot of drinks

PEARY PUNCH

Influential boozologist and author CHRISTINE SISMONDO is a purveyor and lover of fine cocktails and their history. We suggest adding her books *Mondo Cocktail: A Shaken and Stirred History* and *America Walks Into a Bar: A Spirited History of Taverns, and Saloons, Speakeasies and Grog Shops* to your reading list. Her Peary Punch will appeal to cocktail lovers as well as to more traditional wine-only types. It's based on Caribou, the staple French-Canadian winter carnival beverage, but is named after a dying breed: the peary caribou, a subspecies that is smaller and has lighter fur than other caribou. The swap of Riesling instead of the traditional red wine is a superb twist. And, as Christine says, "As an added bonus, it makes your house smell awesome."

1 bottle (750 mL) Niagara Riesling
1 cup Victoria Spirits Victoria Gin
3 whole star anise pods
3 cloves
6 juniper berries
¼ cup chopped ginger
¼ cup maple syrup, or to taste
4 to 6 dashes Bittered Sling Orange and
    Juniper bitters
Freshly grated nutmeg, for garnish

Pour all ingredients except bitters and garnish into a saucepan. Slowly warm over a low heat for 30 minutes. Pour into mugs, leaving solids in saucepan. Add a dash of bitters to each drink and garnish with nutmeg.
Makes 4 to 6 drinks

CHRISTINE'S TIP
This is a forgiving recipe, so feel free to tweak to your liking.

NORTH OF 44

AJA SAX was born in Kelowna, grew up in California and says that some of her most formative cocktail experiences were had in Vancouver—but she's built her impressive bartending career at some of Toronto's most respected bars and restaurants. Starting out under the watchful eye of Dave Mitton, she now heads up and trains her own bar teams. She has a fun and approachable cocktail style, which this drink emulates perfectly. This frothy, velvety, pale pink cocktail tastes just as good as it looks.

2 oz Dillon's Small Batch Distillers
    Unfiltered Gin 22
1 oz freshly squeezed ruby red grapefruit juice
½ oz Riesling Syrup
3 dashes Bittered Sling Grapefruit and
    Hops bitters
¾ oz or 1 small egg white
Large handful of ice cubes

Pour all ingredients except ice into a cocktail shaker. Shake until incorporated and frothy. Add ice and shake until chilled. Double strain through a Hawthorne strainer and a fine-mesh strainer into a chilled coupe glass.
Makes 1 drink

> *Riesling Syrup* <

Pour ½ cup Norman Hardie Riesling and ½ cup granulated sugar in a small saucepan. Set over medium heat. Stirring constantly, gently heat until sugar is dissolved, 5 to 7 minutes. Remove from heat. Pour into a 1-cup sterilized jar with a new lid and ring. Syrup will keep, sealed and refrigerated, for up to 1 week. Makes 6 oz (¾ cup), for 12 drinks

CELERY RICKEY

Jen Agg's Hoof Cocktail Bar is an institution in Toronto, and her British-import bar manager David Greig helps keep it ahead of the game. They serve inventive craft cocktails featuring homemade amaro, bitters, liqueurs and infusions, and we are thrilled to share their Celery Rickey. It uses verjus, a slightly acidic sour-sweet juice that's made from unripened wine grapes. Since verjus is not fermented, it's non-alcoholic, but nevertheless a lovely addition to cocktails.

1 ½ oz gin
4 tsp Celery-Verjus Shrub (see below)
4 tsp freshly squeezed lime juice
½ tsp green Chartreuse
5 drops saline
Large handful of ice cubes
Crushed ice
¼ cup + 1 Tbsp chilled club soda
Celery ribbon, for garnish

Pour all ingredients except ice, soda and garnish into a cocktail shaker. Add handful of ice and shake until chilled. Strain through a Hawthorne strainer into a chilled collins glass filled with crushed ice. Top with soda. Using a vegetable peeler, pull a strip from a celery stalk. Garnish drink with celery ribbon, stir and serve.
Makes 1 drink

> *Celery-Verjus Shrub* <

Preheat the oven to 200°F. Pour 2 cups Ontario Pinot Noir verjus into a small saucepan. Add 2 ½ cups granulated sugar. Set over medium heat. Stir occasionally until sugar is dissolved, about 8 minutes. Meanwhile, chop ½ bunch celery. Place in a medium ovenproof dish. Pour syrup overtop. Bake in centre of the preheated oven for 2 hours. Remove from oven and strain, discarding solids. Strain through a funnel lined with a coffee filter or several layers of cheesecloth into a sterilized jar. Shrub will keep well, sealed and refrigerated, for 2 weeks. Makes at least 26 oz (3 cups), for a lot of drinks

> *Saline* <

Pour 1 cup water and 1 tsp coarse sea salt into a small saucepan. Set over medium heat. Stirring occasionally, heat until salt is dissolved, about 8 minutes. Makes 8 oz (1 cup), for a lot of drinks

THE CANADIAN R&R

Rest and relax with this pretty pink twist on a Rum & Coke. Since rhubarb has a natural affinity for flavours traditionally found in cola—think citrus and pepper—we subbed out the pop of the classic version for our rum and rhubarb twist.

Handful of ice cubes

2 oz white rum, such as Proof or Havana Club

1 lime

2 oz Rhubarb-Peppercorn Syrup (page 183)

1 oz chilled club soda or soda water

1 dash Twisted & Bitter Black Pepper bitters (optional)

1 dash orange bitters (optional)

1 rhubarb curl, for garnish

Fill a chilled old-fashioned glass with ice. Pour in rum. Squeeze in juice of half the lime through a fine-mesh strainer. Using a barspoon, stir until chilled. Continue adding ingredients, and stirring to mix and chill. Cut a wedge from remaining half lime. Garnish drink with lime wedge and rhubarb curl.

Makes 1 drink

RHUBARB GARNISH
Use a vegetable peeler to pull thin strips from rhubarb.
Place in a bowl filled with ice water. Refrigerate until curled, 30 minutes.

PRINCE EDWARD BOUNTY

We like to think of the grainy mustard at the base of this drink as reminiscent of what you might see on the bottom of your glass when picnicking on one of Canada's many beautiful sandy beaches. The surprising addition of mustard and the use of herbal, vegetal aquavit make this cocktail deceivingly good. This drink is a toast to the bountiful produce and flavours that hail from Ontario's foodie haven, Prince Edward County, where the magnificent beach of Sandbanks Provincial Park is located.

2 oz chilled dry white wine, such as Vidal, Pinot Gris or Sauvignon Blanc
½ oz aquavit, such as Aalborg Jubilaeums Akvavit
½ oz Cinnamon Syrup (page 182)
1 tsp St-Germain Elderflower Liqueur
½ tsp mustard seeds or ⅛ tsp Kozlik's Triple Crunch Mustard
Large handful of ice cubes

Pour all ingredients except ice into a cocktail shaker. Add ice and shake until chilled.
Double strain through a Hawthorne strainer and a fine-mesh strainer into a chilled coupe glass.
Makes 1 drink

Canadian Mustard

⋆⋙◎ ◎⋘⋆

Canada produces a range of fantastic mustards—like Kozlik's and its Triple Crunch, featured here, and Amazing Maple—and is one of the largest mustard and mustard seed distributors in the world.

CANADIAN RYE DIRTY MARTINI

DAVIN DE KERGOMMEAUX is the Canadian whisky expert who wrote the fascinating and historically comprehensive book dedicated to the nation's most infamous spirit. So it threw us for a loop when he submitted a vodka martini recipe but, of course, being a constant champion of his favourite grain, he calls for rye vodka. Make this drink before curling up with your copy of *Canadian Whisky: The Portable Expert*, a book any spirit-loving Canadian ought to own.

3 to 4 large ice cubes or 1 handful of ice cubes
2 ½ oz 66 Gilead Distillery Canadian Rye Vodka
½ oz olive brine
Scant ½ oz dry white vermouth
1 green olive, for garnish

Place ice into a mixing glass. Add all ingredients except garnish. Stir until chilled. Strain through a julep strainer into a chilled martini glass. Garnish with olive.

Makes 1 drink

THE ALCHEMIST

Bar manager and co-owner of Montreal cocktail hot spot Le Lab Comptoir à Cocktails, GABRIELLE PANACCIO can rightly claim the title of her cocktail. She loves experimenting with contradictory flavours, and at Le Lab they take a scientific approach to dissecting ingredients to create well-balanced drinks. The maple and mint complement the flavours of the Quebec-made gin, which exhibits parsnip as a major ingredient.

1 ½ oz Les Distillateurs Subversifs Piger
    Henricus Gin
1 oz freshly squeezed lime juice
½ oz maple syrup
8 mint leaves, plus 1 leaf for garnish
2 handfuls of ice cubes
4 oz chilled Perrier
1 Caramelized Parsnip, for garnish

Pour all ingredients except ice, Perrier and garnish into a cocktail shaker. Add 1 handful of ice and shake well for 8 to 10 seconds. Fine strain into a chilled old-fashioned glass filled with remaining ice. Garnish with caramelized parsnip slice and fresh mint leaf.

Makes 1 drink

> *Caramelized Parsnip* <

Preheat the oven to 375°F. Cut a peeled parsnip lengthwise into long thin pieces no thicker than ½ inch. In a bowl, mix together 1 Tbsp maple syrup, 1 tsp olive oil and a pinch of salt. Add parsnip, turning to coat. Spread on a baking sheet. Bake in centre of the preheated oven, turning pieces halfway through cooking time, until parsnip is caramelized, about 20 minutes. Makes enough for several drinks.

CARIBOU

Caribou is a robust fortified wine–based beverage made famous by Quebec City's annual winter carnival, where it is often sipped from long red canes. Caribou can be purchased by the bottle or made at home. Many versions involve a mix of wine or fortified wine, spirit, spices and maple syrup, which can make it almost mulled wine–like. It can be enjoyed warm or cold. We played around with flavours until we arrived at this robust and spicy version, which can be likened to a Sangarée.

2 oz Cabernet Sauvignon
1 oz Michel Jodoin Calijo or calvados
½ oz Maple-Port Reduction
1 dash Dr. Adam Elmegirab's Dandelion and
   Burdock Bitters
Large handful of ice cubes
1 orange peel strip

Combine ingredients except ice and orange peel into a mixing glass. Add ice and stir gently until chilled. Strain through a julep strainer into a chilled coupe glass or port glass. Pull a long strip of orange peel over the glass, releasing oils into cocktail. Gently pinch, peel side out, misting oils over surface of the drink. Rub peel around the outside rim of the glass, then add. Makes 1 drink

> *Maple-Port Reduction* <

Pour 1 ½ cups port and ½ cup maple syrup into a small saucepan. Bring to a vigorous simmer over medium-high heat. Reduce heat to medium-low and simmer mixture for 30 to 35 minutes, until reduced to about ⅔ cup. If you're making drinks for a crowd, this recipe is easily doubled. Reduction will keep, sealed and refrigerated, for 2 weeks. Makes 5 oz (⅔ cup), for 10 drinks

VICTORIA'S SHORTCUT
No time to make the maple-port reduction?
Use ½ oz port and 1 tsp maple syrup in its place.

THE POLAR VORTEX

RYAN GRAY worked at some of Montreal's most top-notch spots, including Joe Beef, before becoming co-owner of the reputable Nora Gray. We are delighted to share here one of his original drinks, named after the notorious cold snap. It's designed, he says, "to warm you up upon arrival at our little restaurant after braving the sub-zero temperatures."

¾ oz Canadian Club Small Batch Classic 12
¾ oz Vecchio Amaro del Capo
½ oz freshly squeezed lemon juice
½ oz apple juice, preferably Quebec-made
¼ oz Apple Syrup
2 dashes Coster's Prescription Coffee and
   A Smoke Bitters
Handful of ice cubes
1 apple, for garnish
1 cinnamon stick, for garnish

Pour all ingredients except ice and garnishes into a mixing glass. Add ice and stir until chilled. Strain through a Hawthorne strainer into a chilled coupe glass. Garnish with apple peel and cinnamon stick.

Makes 1 drink

> *Apple Syrup* <

Pour 1 cup Quebec apple juice into a medium saucepan. Set over medium heat. Simmer until reduced to ¼ cup, about 25 minutes. Remove from heat and let cool completely. Syrup will keep, sealed and refrigerated, for at least 1 week. Makes 2 oz (¼ cup), for 8 drinks

AMARO

If you can't get your hands on the amaro Ryan calls for,
Amaro Averna will do the trick.

SAISON ROYALE

Co-owner of Hotel Herman, DOMINIC GOYET pays special attention to pairing food and drink, which helps inspire his innovative cocktail menus. In his Saison Royale, Dominic strikes a delightful balance between sweet and sour. We adore the addition of Saison du Tracteur—from Shawinigan's outstanding Microbrasserie Le Trou du Diable—which imparts a complex, fruity and spicy froth to this cocktail.

½ lemon
½ oz Simple Syrup (page 182)
2 oz calvados
1 whole egg
Large handful of ice cubes
2 oz chilled Microbrasserie Le Trou du
    Diable Saison du Tracteur beer

Muddle lemon with simple syrup into a cocktail shaker. Add calvados and egg. Shake until frothy, about 20 seconds. Add ice and shake until chilled, about 20 more seconds. Double strain through a Hawthorne strainer and a fine-mesh strainer into a chilled cognac glass. Top with beer.
Makes 1 drink

THE BOREAL COTTON-CANDY COCKTAIL

The aroma of balsam fir conjures up memories of a walk through the woods. So it's pretty surprising that the flavour of the syrup in this frothy drink is more likely to remind you of cotton candy. Balsam fir syrup is a must-try for diehard locavores and foraged-goods fans alike. Balsam fir grows abundantly in Canada, particularly in dense forests like the boreal. Not a forager? You can order balsam fir tips online.

¾ oz or 1 small egg white
1 ½ oz vodka, such as Pur Vodka
¾ oz Blue Curacao
1 oz Balsam Fir Syrup (page 183)
1 ¼ oz freshly squeezed lime juice
Large handful of ice cubes
Splash chilled club soda

Pour all ingredients except ice and soda into a cocktail shaker. Dry shake until incorporated and frothy. Add ice and shake until chilled. Double strain through a Hawthorne strainer and a fine-mesh strainer into a large chilled champagne flute or collins glass. Top with soda. Gently stir to mix.

Makes 1 drink

BOTTLE BASICS

Retro-associated electrically coloured liqueurs have been making a comeback as of late, if only in celebration of irony. We used Blue Curacao for its citrus-spiked flavour but mostly for its cotton-candy colour.

SWEET FERN G&T

Sweet fern—not actually a fern but an herb—lends a very delicate and interesting taste to a cocktail. To get your hands on it, keep your eyes peeled at your local farmers' market, or order it online. Homemade sweet fern–infused tonic makes for a standout, refreshing drink that is sure to win over classic G&T diehards. You may also convert those who have sworn them off!

1 ½ to 2 oz gin	Add gin and Sweet Fern Tonic Syrup to an
¾ oz Sweet Fern Tonic Syrup	ice-filled chilled old-fashioned glass. Top with
Handful of ice cubes	soda. Squeeze in juice from lime wedge.
3 oz chilled club soda	Stir until chilled.
1 lime wedge	Makes 1 drink

> *Sweet Fern Tonic Syrup* <

Sweet fern (*Comptonia peregrina*) is a fragrant wild herb native to the Boreal Shield and the mixed wood plains of Central and Eastern Canada. In addition to being used as incense, thanks to its fragrance, it's used to treat poison ivy and is often consumed as a tea by northerners for its tonic properties. It seemed like a perfect, more pleasantly flavoured alternative to cinchona bark, the traditional bittering agent used to make tonic water.

1 grapefruit	1 cup water
1 lime	¼ cup coarsely crumbled dried
1 cup granulated sugar	sweet fern leaves and stems

Using a rasp, zest ½ tsp peel from grapefruit and ¼ tsp peel from lime. Place sugar and water in a small saucepan (choose one that has a tight-fitting lid). Set over medium heat. Bring to a boil, stirring occasionally. Remove from heat. When bubbling subsides, finely crumble sweet fern into syrup. Add grapefruit and lime zest. Stir to distribute evenly. Cover saucepan with lid and let stand for 10 minutes to allow flavours to infuse. Uncover and let cool for 10 minutes. Fine strain through a funnel lined with a coffee filter or several layers of cheesecloth into a sterilized jar with a tight-fitting lid. Syrup will keep, sealed and refrigerated, for 2 weeks. Makes 10 oz (1 ¼ cups), for 14 drinks

SAUCIER'S SEIGNIORY SPECIAL

In *Bottoms Up*, Ted Saucier features recipes from some of the most lavish and elite hotel bars in the world. The Seigniory Club (now known as Château Montebello) was, in Ted's time, a private club, and this drink would have been sipped by its rich, famous and politically powerful members. We reworked the classic cocktail to make a beautifully balanced, classy drink that doesn't require membership to enjoy. (See drink photo on page 33.)

1 oz rye whisky, such as Alberta Springs

¾ oz or 1 small egg white

¾ oz maple liqueur, preferably Sortilège Canadian Whisky and Maple Syrup Liqueur

½ oz dark spiced rum, such as The Kraken Black Spiced Rum

½ oz freshly squeezed grapefruit juice

½ oz freshly squeezed lemon juice

1 tsp maple syrup

Large handful of ice cubes

1 grapefruit wisp, for garnish

Pour all ingredients except ice and garnish into a cocktail shaker. Dry shake until incorporated and frothy. Add ice and shake until chilled. Double strain through a Hawthorne strainer and a fine-mesh strainer into a chilled coupe glass. Pull a small wisp of peel from grapefruit over drink. Gently rub wisp around the outside rim of the glass. Cut a small slit in the wisp, then fasten to the glass rim.

Makes 1 drink

BOTTLE BASICS

Quebec has no shortage of liqueurs, cream liqueurs, fortified wines, mistelles, ciders and spirits showcasing the Québécois staple flavour: maple. A quality maple liqueur is a must-have and an excellent addition to fall and wintery cocktails. Sortilège works well in this cocktail because of its complementary whisky base.

BLACK BEAUX-ARTS FIZZ

This velvety, robust cocktail takes inspiration from a drink called the Beaux Arts Fizz (not to be mistaken for a Beaux Arts Cocktail). The Fizz was popular at a certain New York City ladies-only bar—designed to offer women a break from shopping or a place to pop in to before heading to the theatre. We did not find an exact recipe but liked the ingredient list: grenadine, orgeat, lemon juice and gin. We've made our own version with homemade grenadine and orgeat featuring local Quebec ingredients. It seemed fitting to dedicate this Canadian version to the gorgeous Musée des Beaux-Arts in Montreal.

1 very thin lime peel strip
3 blackberries, for garnish
1 ½ oz gin
¾ oz or 1 small egg white
¾ oz Blackberry Grenadine (page 189)
¾ oz Black Walnut Orgeat (page 192)
½ oz freshly squeezed lime juice
Large handful of ice cubes

Using a channel knife, pull a very thin strip of peel from lime. Prepare a garnish of blackberries on a cocktail skewer, wrapped with lime strip. Pour all ingredients except garnish and ice into a cocktail shaker. Shake until incorporated and frothy. Add ice and shake until chilled. Double strain through a Hawthorne strainer and a fine-mesh strainer into a chilled coupe glass. Garnish with prepared skewer.
Makes 1 drink

EVEN EASIER
If you don't have time to make grenadine and orgeat, simply sub in store-bought versions. The result is a bright pink drink.

LA POMME DU DIABLE

Like the apple that tempted Eve, this drink is impossible to resist. This refreshing, slightly savoury cocktail is a distant relative of an El Diablo but with brilliantly sour-sweet ice cider in place of crème de cassis.

¾ oz Domaine Pinnacle Ice Cider

2 fresh sage leaves

1 ½ oz blanco tequila

¼ oz green Chartreuse

¼ oz freshly squeezed lime juice

3 dashes The Bitter Truth Celery Bitters

Large handful of ice cubes

Crushed ice

2 oz chilled ginger beer

Place ice cider and 1 sage leaf in a cocktail shaker and muddle sage gently. Add remaining ingredients except ice and ginger beer. Add ice cubes and shake until chilled. Double strain through a Hawthorne strainer and a fine-mesh strainer into a chilled collins glass filled with crushed ice. Top with ginger beer. Smack remaining sage leaf, rub around the outside rim of the glass, then add. Stir lightly with a straw.
Makes 1 drink

BOTTLE BASICS

The attractive natural hue of Chartreuse inspired the name of a colour. It doesn't just look magical; this digestif is enchantingly potent and intensely herbaceous, prepared as it is with 130 botanicals. French monks have been producing this vibrant liqueur since the seventeenth century, guarding the recipe closely.

The
EAST

RECIPES IN THIS SECTION:

FIDDLEHEAD MARTINI

THE LOYALIST

THE COUPE DE CARTIER

ACADIAN DRIFTWOOD

MAGNETIC HILL SOUR

THE BRIGHT RED

SPARKLING WATERMELON SIPPER

THE NELLIE J. BANKS

WILD ROSE NEGRONI

THE POST SUNSET

LAVENDER-BLUEBERRY SPARKLER

WINTER GARDEN

PUMPKIN COLADA

1749 NEGRONI

THE CORRODED NAIL

HOT BUTTERED RUM

COLD BUTTERED RUM

LABRADOR ICED TEA

ST. JOHN'S SLING

THE 52%

NAN'S KITCHEN

The next stop on our cocktail journey brings us to the Atlantic provinces, known for their welcoming hospitality and friendliness—an honourable reputation that's reaffirmed every time we visit. Common pleasantries are infectious, and there's something about the landscape that always makes you feel at home, whether you're driving from town to town or having a night out in the city.

We embarked on an East Coast getaway to join a family trip celebrating Scott's parents' fortieth wedding anniversary on Prince Edward Island, taking the opportunity to combine the celebration with a cocktail pilgrimage. We took New Brunswick's scenic Acadian Coastal Drive to maximize our time oceanside, making a detour to Petit-Paquetville to visit the reputable Distillerie Fils du Roy. Sadly, it was undergoing renovations and was closed, but we did find its product in a tiny New Brunswick liquor store, which had a whole shelf devoted entirely to Fils du Roy. Other local shoppers were quick to tell us about distiller Sébastien Roy's incredible spirits, and about the prestigious awards he's been accumulating. His products are masterfully crafted. Find them in our Fiddlehead Martini (page 139) and Coupe de Cartier (page 141).

We built in extra time and drove toward Saint John to stay with friends.

New Brunswick highlights include relaxing with refreshing sours on the patio of the Tide and Boar in Moncton (see recipe, page 144), and grabbing a variety of interesting beers from Picaroons Brewing Company in Fredericton. If you're heading that way, we recommend taking the gorgeous drive along the Bay of Fundy, a spectacular coastline with the highest tides in the world. Make sure to get out of the car and explore; hunting for tiny crabs at low tide in Fundy National Park and poking around the Hopewell Rocks were unforgettable moments for us. If you're heading toward PEI, make sure to stop at Winegarden Estate. This fruit winery and distillery, en route to the Confederation Bridge, has been producing spirits, liqueurs and wines for decades. Many of its products are available widely in the East, like its superb Johnny Ziegler Brandy and its maple liqueur, but at the distillery you can sample more offerings, including bitters and bitter liqueurs.

Once we crossed Confederation Bridge into PEI, we pulled over to watch the sunset. At this point, we had officially switched over to island time. Later that evening, we were pleased to discover that a common way to pass that time is to enjoy drinks by a campfire on the beach. In the days to follow, we indulged in a fabulous lobster boil—

an East Coast pastime—with family and friends. We spent the day in Charlottetown picking up goods for a blissful week of feasting. We grabbed cheese and other delicacies at Terre Rouge, where we were introduced to John Pritchard's Wild Rose Negroni (page 150), then we headed to the Charlottetown Farmers' Market to knock everything else off our grocery list. Later, we incorporated some of our finds in the first incarnation of the flaming tiki–style cocktail, the Nellie J. Banks (page 148). The cocktail features products from Myriad View Artisan Distillery—its moonshine-inspired spirits are a fun nod to Prohibition, which lasted longer on Prince Edward Island than in any other province. Props go to John Rossignol, owner of Rossignol Estate Winery, who spearheaded the first commercial winery in PEI, overcoming previously strict laws dating back to Prohibition. There are now several wineries and a few distilleries, and many places, including Matos Winery, are experimenting on both fronts. We were very impressed by their Portuguese-influenced spirit bagaço, and their Angelica, featured in our Sparkling Watermelon Sipper (page 147). Pair this sparkling cocktail with Canadian oysters, which PEI has no shortage of (see oyster guide, page 194).

After a relaxing time on the island, we were craving a bit of city life, so we continued to Halifax. There's a lot to do in the city, and since things are fairly concentrated, we left the car parked and celebrated our own wedding anniversary with early afternoon drinks at the Bicycle Thief (check out Jeffrey Van Horne's recipe, page 158). Afterward, we meandered around the waterfront, watching playful seals and exploring Bishop's Landing. Victoria was thrilled to get a small chunk of Fox Hill Cheese House Fenugreek Havarti cheese at Halifax Seaport Farmers' Market. This almost-maple-tasting fromage is a favourite from past visits and tough to get a hold of back home. We spent the evening in the North End, picking up charcuterie at Ratinaud French Cuisine for a picnic, then sampling beers at Propeller Brewing Company. For dinner we had unforgettable scallops on the shell with classic cocktails and rosé at Edna. Halifax has a tight cocktail scene. Renowned spots include Noble, the Drawing Room and Field Guide (see bartender Shane Beehan's Winter Garden recipe, page 155). Some places are open only on the weekends, so plan accordingly.

You can either make Halifax your home base for the duration of your stay in Nova Scotia—making a few day trips to outlying towns—or pick up and travel around. We recommend heading south to Lunenburg and the Ironworks Distillery. Go for a winery tour of the Annapolis Valley, enjoy tastings and have dinner along the way. If you're Cabot Trail bound, try visiting Nova Scotia's northernmost winery, Eileanan Brèagha Vineyards, and make sure to stop by or stay at Glenora Inn and Distillery. You can taste tradition at Louisburg National Historic Site with a glass of Authentic Seacoast Distilling Company Ltd.'s Fortress Rum, which is aged in barrels on site. And the Cape Breton Farmers' Market in Sydney is a great spot to find lots of island-made beauties, including beer from Big Spruce Brewing. You could even use Big Spruce's Tip of the Spear Spruce IPA to make a classic Atlantic cocktail, the Calibogus—a simple mix of dark rum and spruce beer. From Cape Breton, you can catch the ferry to Newfoundland. We've dedicated one of our cocktails to that ride, including our favourite ingredients from the two linked provinces (see The Corroded Nail, page 159).

Have you ever kissed a cod? If you've been to Newfoundland, you likely have. This unusual welcoming tradition involves a "screech-in" ceremony and, yes, kissing a fish. But this is not the only thing special to Newfoundland; its profound beauty and island lifestyle

are remarkable. Scott's been and had an incredible time, so we have a shortlist of activities for a future trip. We plan to go on a hike to the Ferryland lighthouse, boat over to Fogo Island to try cocktails at the Fogo Island Inn (see bar manager Jacob Luksic's recipe, page 166) and visit a few Newfoundland wineries (yes, there are a handful there), where wines made from crow-, cloud- and partridge berries are common. There is even some evidence to suggest that the province may be home to the first ever vineyards on Canadian shores, dating back to Viking days. We are looking forward to travelling the island and Labrador together some day, but for now we'll sip on the St. John's Sling (page 164), made with the local favourite, screech rum.

It wouldn't be right to talk about the East Coast—especially in the context of drinking!—and not mention kitchen parties. They are common practice in the eastern provinces, often involving impromptu jam sessions as friends gather to party in the comfort of their own kitchens. We've included a few big-batch and punch options in this chapter for such occasions, plus an eclectic collection of East Coast–inspired cocktails so you can revel in the Atlantic spirit in your own kitchen, wherever that may be.

FIDDLEHEAD MARTINI

Fiddleheads are a springtime favourite throughout Canada, especially in New Brunswick. The province's River Valley Scenic Drive is symbolized by a fiddlehead; Tide Head proudly calls itself the "Fiddlehead Capital of the World"; a giant stone fiddlehead statue stands outside the Saint John Arts Centre; and New Brunswick's best-known literary magazine, which has been published for nearly seventy years, is titled *The Fiddlehead*. Welcome warmer weather with this bright, crisp, classic martini garnished with a fiddlehead.

2 oz gin or vodka, preferably Distillerie Fils du
   Roy Gin Thuya or Grande Bagosse
¼ to ½ oz dry vermouth
Large handful of ice cubes
1 Lemony Pickled Fiddlehead (optional)
1 lemon peel strip (optional)

Pour gin and vermouth into a mixing glass. If using Gin Thuya, we suggest ¼ oz vermouth, as this gin carries extra floral and fruit notes. Add ice and stir until chilled, approximately 50 swirls or 45 seconds. Strain through a julep strainer into a chilled martini glass. Garnish with a pickled fiddlehead. If you aren't garnishing with the pickled fiddlehead or you like extra lemony flavour, pull a long strip of lemon peel over the glass, releasing oils into cocktail. Gently pinch, peel side out, misting oils over surface of the drink. Rub peel around outside rim of the glass, then add.

Makes 1 drink

> *Lemony Pickled Fiddleheads* <

Trim ends and remove brown papery bits from 2 cups or ¼ lb fresh fiddleheads. Fill a large bowl with cold water. Soak to release dirt and debris. Scoop out and remove any papery bits. Carefully remove fiddleheads, leaving settled dirt on the bottom. Repeat process, rinsing and refilling with fresh cold water until clean. Drain well and pat dry with paper towels.

Bring large pan partially filled with water to a boil. Add fiddleheads. Cook just until fork tender, 1 to 2 minutes. Immediately plunge into a bowl of ice water. Let cool completely, then drain well. Add 3 long strips of lemon peel to a jar. Pack in prepared fiddleheads. Place ⅔ cup white wine vinegar, ⅔ cup water, 2 tsp coarse kosher salt, 1 tsp granulated sugar, 1 tsp whole black peppercorns and 1 bay leaf in a small saucepan. Set over medium heat. Heat until steaming and salt and sugar are dissolved, 3 to 5 minutes. Pour mixture over fiddleheads, leaving ½ inch headspace in jar. Seal jar tightly. Refrigerate overnight to allow flavours to infuse. Will keep, sealed and refrigerated, for at least 1 to 2 weeks. Makes 16 oz (2 cups)

THE LOYALIST

In the late eighteenth century, the population of New Brunswick (then part of Nova Scotia) exploded, basically quadrupling. British Loyalists fleeing America were welcomed and even given acreage to help set up and establish the new country of Canada. As Loyalists were given governing offices and titles, the move for an independent province was born. This aperitif combines the British influence of London dry gin with a local NB favourite: sweet-and-sour wild blueberries, a perfect complement to Campari's bitterness. Despite the fine straining called for in this recipe, some berry pulp will remain in the drink. But it works—we like the subtle grittiness that makes the cocktail reminiscent of an Old-Fashioned.

3 Tbsp blueberries, preferably wild
1 oz Lillet Blanc
1 oz Campari
1 oz London dry gin, such as Beefeater
Large handful of ice cubes
1 large ice cube
1 orange peel strip

Muddle blueberries with Lillet in a cocktail shaker. Add Campari and gin, then handful of ice cubes. Shake just until chilled. Double strain through a Hawthorne strainer and a fine-mesh strainer over large ice cube in an old-fashioned glass. Pull a long strip of orange peel over the glass, releasing oils into cocktail. Gently pinch, peel side out, misting oils over surface of the drink. Rub peel around the outside rim of the glass, then add.

Makes 1 drink

THE COUPE DE CARTIER

Jacques Cartier may not have had such a lasting experience when he landed at Baie des Chaleurs were it not for the help of the Iroquois, who aided in the settlement of New France by teaching the French the lay of the land, and by famously providing a surprise cure for the scurvy-ridden bunch. The fragrant, vitamin-rich eastern white cedar is abundant if somewhat underappreciated, but now Distillerie Fils du Roy makes the new-age-style Gin Thuya, flavoured with that same cedar. The Courailleuse (absinthe) adds great depth to this variation on a Bee's Knees while acknowledging the French influence of the region.

2 oz gin, preferably Distillerie Fils du
    Roy Gin Thuya
¾ oz Honey Syrup (page 183)
½ oz freshly squeezed lemon juice
Absinthe, such as Distillerie Fils du
    Roy La Courailleuse or Pernod, for rinse
Large handful of ice cubes

Pour gin, honey syrup and lemon juice into a cocktail shaker. Rinse a chilled coupe glass with absinthe. Add ice to a shaker and shake until chilled. Double strain through a Hawthorne strainer and a fine-mesh strainer into the prepared glass.

Makes 1 drink

ACADIAN DRIFTWOOD

This liquor-forward Scotch cocktail encapsulates Acadian-inspired flavours, including maple whisky and a balsam fir syrup, creating a perfectly balanced drink with a foresty feel. It's best sipped fireside on a cold winter night.

1 ½ oz smoky single malt Islay Scotch, such as Laphroaig Quarter Cask
¾ oz maple whisky liqueur, such as Sortilège Canadian Whisky and Maple Syrup Liqueur
½ oz sweet red vermouth
¼ oz Balsam Fir Syrup (page 183)
1 dash Bittered Sling Moondog bitters or Angostura bitters
Handful of ice cubes
1 lemon twist, for garnish

Pour all ingredients except ice and garnish into a mixing glass. Add ice and stir until chilled. Strain through a julep strainer into a chilled coupe glass. Pull a small twist of peel from lemon over drink. Gently rub twist around the outside rim of the glass. Cut a small slit in the twist, then fasten to the glass rim.

Makes 1 drink

FUN FACT

The balsam fir is the provincial tree of New Brunswick.

MAGNETIC HILL SOUR

CHAD STEEVES is responsible for this sour, made with a combination of whisky and Magnetic Hill Winery dessert wine. It's perfect for enjoying on a patio, like we did at his Tide and Boar gastropub in Moncton.

1 oz Canadian Club Reserve Whisky
¾ oz freshly squeezed lemon juice
½ oz Simple Syrup (page 182)
¼ oz freshly squeezed lime juice
Large handful of ice cubes
Crushed ice
2 oz Magnetic Hill Winery Raspberry
    Dessert Wine

Pour all ingredients except ice and wine into a cocktail shaker. Add ice cubes and shake for about 15 seconds. Strain into a chilled double old-fashioned glass filled with crushed ice. Carefully pour in the dessert wine near the edge of the drink. It may sink to the bottom, creating an ombré effect.

Makes 1 drink

TRAVEL TIP

Moncton's Magnetic Hill became famous in the 1960s for its optical illusion whereby cars in neutral gear appear to coast uphill in reverse. If you're visiting the area, make sure to stop in at Magnetic Hill Winery to pick up its raspberry dessert wine.

THE BRIGHT RED

This is our tribute to the young, pigtailed, red-headed protagonist of Lucy Maud Montgomery's cherished Canadian novel, *Anne of Green Gables*. The tale of Anne's best friend, Diana, enjoying too much raspberry cordial—which the two girls believed to be non-alcoholic but turned out to be blackcurrant wine—inspired this drink. We've combined homemade raspberry cordial (a boozy version) with red wine.

1 ½ oz red wine
¾ oz Raspberry Cordial (page 190) or
    raspberry liqueur, such as Chambord
½ oz freshly squeezed lemon juice
½ oz Simple Syrup (page 182)
Large handful of ice cubes
2 oz chilled club soda

Pour all ingredients except ice and soda into a cocktail shaker. Add ice and shake until chilled. Double strain through a Hawthorne strainer and a fine-mesh strainer into a chilled red wine glass. Top with soda.

Makes 1 drink

VARIATION

For a modern twist, make use of trendy pisco and Lillet
by using ¾ oz of each in place of the red wine.

SPARKLING WATERMELON SIPPER

Watermelon and oysters pair beautifully, so we conjured up this effervescent pink melon cocktail to enjoy with our favourite bivalves.

6 watermelon cubes, each 1 inch

2 oz Matos Winery & Distillery Angelica or ¾ oz Dry Curacao

¼ oz freshly squeezed lemon juice

Large handful of ice cubes

6 oz chilled sparkling wine or vinho verde

Place watermelon into a cocktail shaker. Pour in Angelica and lemon juice. Muddle watermelon. Add ice and shake until chilled. Double strain through a Hawthorne strainer and a fine-mesh strainer into a measuring cup. Carefully divide between 2 champagne flutes. Top each with sparkling wine.

Makes 2 drinks

FOOD PAIRINGS

This sparkler is superb served with PEI oysters, of course. It's also a fantastic accompaniment to local cheese, such as PEI's Cheese Lady's Gouda.

THE NELLIE J. BANKS

Although PEI was the first province to accept strict Prohibition in 1901, it was also a big player in the rum-running game, helping to keep the illegal hooch flowing throughout Canada and to our southerly neighbours. The *Nellie J. Banks* was the longest surviving rum-running ship from Prince Edward Island. She was given a spectacular burial in 1953 by being set ablaze and sent to sea. We drew inspiration from the rum-running stories of the past to create this island tiki–style cocktail that gets flamed as a tribute to *Nellie J.*

1 lime
1 lemon
1 oz Myriad View Artisan Distillery Strait
    Rum or overproof amber rum
¾ oz Myriad View Artisan Distillery Strait
    Shine or Wray & Nephew white rum
¾ oz Rich Blueberry Syrup (page 183)
3 to 4 dashes Angostura bitters
Large handful of ice cubes
Crushed ice
2 oz chilled club soda
¼ oz Myriad View Artisan Distillery Strait
    Lightning or ½ oz Bacardi 151
Generous pinch freshly grated cinnamon

Cut lime in half crosswise. Squeeze and strain ½ oz juice each from lime and lemon, reserving shell of lime for garnish. Using a grapefruit spoon, carve out pulp from remaining lime half. Place juices, rum, shine, blueberry syrup and bitters into a cocktail shaker. Add ice cubes and shake until chilled. Strain into a wide-mouth, heatproof tiki mug filled with crushed ice. Pour soda overtop.

Have a heatproof saucer at hand to put out the flame. Float prepared half lime on surface of the drink. Pour Lightning into lime boat and using a barbecue lighter, ignite. Carefully sprinkle cinnamon lightly overtop. Let flame spread over surface of lime boat for no more than 10 seconds. Carefully place saucer over mouth of cup to extinguish flame. Tip over lime boat with a straw and stir to evenly mix. Let glass rim cool before serving.

Makes 1 drink big enough for sharing

BOTTLE BASICS

Aside from the illegal route, the only way to get hooch in PEI in the early twentieth century was by doctor's orders. We love the irony that one of the co-owners of the Myriad View Artisan Distillery happened to be a local doctor. Alongside its moonshine-esque spirits, the distillery also experiments with other spirits, like their Strait Gin.

WILD ROSE NEGRONI

Chef and co-owner of Terre Rouge, JOHN PRITCHARD mans the front of house at this locally focused restaurant in Charlottetown. There you can enjoy classic drinks with regional twists. This one is almost a classic Negroni, but it makes use of wild rose liqueur from Rossignol Estate Winery. Pritchard favours the winery's liqueur over vermouth, as they have parallel flavour profiles but the liqueur is fragrant.

1 oz gin
1 oz Campari
1 oz Rossignol Estate Winery Wild Rose Liqueur
1 to 2 handfuls of ice cubes
1 orange peel strip

Pour gin, Campari and liqueur into a mixing glass. Add 1 handful of ice cubes and stir until chilled. Strain through a julep strainer into a chilled old-fashioned glass. Serve over a second handful of ice cubes, if you like. Pull a long strip of orange peel over the glass, releasing oils into cocktail. Gently pinch, peel side out, misting oils over surface of the drink. Rub peel around the outside rim of the glass, then add.
Makes 1 drink

Classic Negroni

You can follow these instructions to build yourself a classic Negroni too.
Simply sub in sweet red vermouth for the wild rose liqueur.

THE POST SUNSET

JENNER CORMIER has travelled to and lived in various places across Canada, but he grew up in Nova Scotia, and he still calls it home. It's there that he earned a reputation for his carefully crafted drinks at some fantastic Halifax bars, such as Noble, before winning Canada's Best Bartender in the Diageo Class 2013 competition—a spot he claimed with this lovely and balanced drink.

2 lime wedges
1 oz freshly squeezed blood orange or
    navel orange juice
¾ oz Aperol
½ oz Limoncello
1 ¼ oz blanco tequila, such as Don Julio Blanco
Large handful of ice cubes
1 ½ to 2 oz chilled Prosecco
1 thinly sliced small lime wheel, preferably
    dehydrated, for garnish

Squeeze juice from lime wedges into a cocktail shaker. Add remaining ingredients except ice, Prosecco and garnish. Add ice and shake until chilled. Double strain through a Hawthorne strainer and a fine-mesh strainer into a chilled large champagne flute. Top with Prosecco. Garnish with lime wheel.
Makes 1 drink

LAVENDER-BLUEBERRY SPARKLER

Floral and delicately fragrant lavender balanced by the distinct sweet-tart flavour of blueberry liqueur make up this elegant coupe cocktail.

1 oz Lavender-Infused Gin (page 184)
¾ oz blueberry liqueur, such as from
    Ironworks Distillery or Distillerie Fils du Roy
¼ oz freshly squeezed lemon juice
¼ oz Simple Syrup (page 182)
Large handful of ice cubes
2 oz chilled sparkling wine
1 fresh lavender sprig, for garnish (optional)

Pour gin, liqueur, lemon juice and simple syrup into a cocktail shaker. Add ice and shake until chilled. Double strain through a Hawthorne strainer and a fine-mesh strainer into a chilled coupe glass. Top with sparkling wine. If using lavender garnish, float overtop.

Makes 1 drink

BOTTLE BASICS

The liqueurs and spirits created by Ironworks Distillery in Lunenburg carry clean, pure-fruit flavours with very subtle sweetness. Standouts include the Pear Eau de Vie and Bluenose Black Rum, as well as the seasonal Rhubarb Esprit.

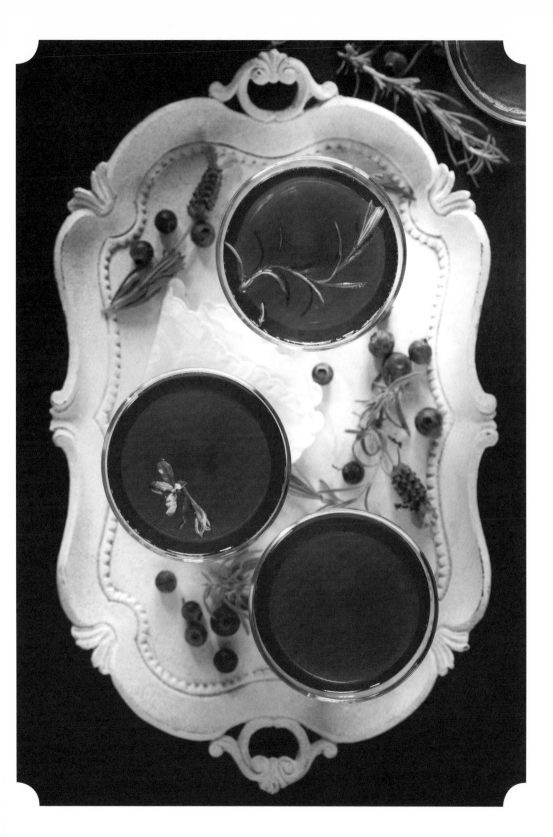

WINTER GARDEN

SHANE BEEHAN sees cocktails as more than just drinks. He believes they are glimpses into culture, society and history. This former student of Atlantic Canadian literature sees creating a drink as an act of poetry, often finding inspiration in the rich history of the Maritimes. His Winter Garden cocktail may help you remember that warm summer feeling on even the coldest of January days.

Scotch, for rinse
1 ½ oz London dry gin
½ oz sweet vermouth
½ oz freshly squeezed lemon juice
½ oz Rich Honey Syrup (page 183)
6 drops rosewater
Large handful of ice cubes
Dried rosebud, for garnish (optional)

Pour all ingredients except ice, Scotch and garnish into a cocktail shaker. Rinse a chilled coupe glass with Scotch. Add ice and shake until chilled. Double strain through a Hawthorne strainer and a fine-mesh strainer into the prepared glass. If using rosebud garnish, float overtop.

Makes 1 drink

PUMPKIN COLADA

Pumpkin season is cause for celebration in Nova Scotia, and loads of pumpkin festivals are held. There are many weigh-offs and community events all over the province, and even an annual pumpkin regatta in Windsor. In case you're wondering, yes, that involves paddling in hollowed-out giant pumpkins. Windsor is the proud home of Howard Dill, who brought the world the largest variety of pumpkin, the Atlantic Giant. This is a Piña Colada variation with the season's best, designed for a group to sip beachside while watching the big orange ships roll in.

8 oz dark spiced rum, such as The Kraken Black Spiced Rum or Ironworks Distillery Bluenose Black Rum

8 oz Coconut Pumpkin Butter or 2 Tbsp each pumpkin purée and coconut cream

6 oz unsweetened pineapple juice

2 oz freshly squeezed orange juice

12 dashes Angostura bitters

4 heaping cups crushed ice

4 homemade cocktail cherries (page 188) or store-bought, for garnish

Tiny pinches grated nutmeg, preferably freshly grated, for garnish

Pour all ingredients except garnishes into a blender. Blend and pulse to an icy-slush consistency, pausing to scrape down sides of blender as needed. Pour into 4 chilled collins glasses. Garnish each with a cherry and sprinkle of nutmeg.

Makes 4 drinks

> *Coconut Pumpkin Butter* <

If using fresh pumpkin, preheat the oven to 400°F. Cut 2 lb fresh pumpkin pieces in half and remove seeds and pulp. If pumpkin is very large, cut once or twice more. Roast in centre of the preheated oven until very soft, about 1 hour. Remove from oven and let cool slightly. Scoop out flesh and place in a blender. Whirl until smooth.

Place puréed pumpkin or 1 can (400 mL) pumpkin purée (not spiced pie filling), ½ cup granulated sugar and 1/8 tsp ground cinnamon in a small saucepan. Set over medium heat. Cook, stirring often, to evaporate some of the water content and create a very thick pumpkin butter. This will take about 20 minutes. Let cool. Whirl in blender until very smooth. Whirl in 1 can (400 mL) coconut cream. Scrape down sides of blender as needed. For the best consistency, use a ladle to press and strain pumpkin mixture through a sieve into a container. Pumpkin butter will keep, sealed and refrigerated, for at least 1 week. Makes 24 oz (3 cups), for 12 drinks

1749 NEGRONI

JEFFREY VAN HORNE was born and raised in Halifax, where he's known for his craft cocktails. This clever drink is his cheers to the birth of Halifax and to Appleton Estate Jamaica Rum—both established in 1749.

1 oz Appleton Estate 12 Year Old Jamaica Rum
1 oz amontillado sherry
1 oz Campari
4 dashes Angostura bitters
Handful of ice cubes
1 large ice cube
1 orange peel strip

Pour all ingredients except ice and orange peel into a mixing glass. Add handful of ice cubes and stir for 30 seconds. Strain through a julep strainer over large ice cube in a chilled old-fashioned glass. Using a peeler, pull a long strip of orange peel over the glass, releasing oils into cocktail. Gently pinch, peel side out, misting oils over surface of the drink. Rub peel around the outside rim of the glass, then add.
Makes 1 drink

THE CORRODED NAIL

We dedicate this variation of the Rusty Nail to the lovely ferry that carries passengers back and forth from Cape Breton Island to Newfoundland, since this easy-going-down drink showcases excellent spirits from both places. (See drink photo on page 33.)

2 oz single malt whisky, such as
   Glen Breton Rare 10 Year
1 oz cloudberry liqueur, such as
   Rodrigues Winery, or apricot liqueur
1 dash orange bitters
Handful of ice cubes
1 large ice cube
1 long orange peel strip

Pour all ingredients except ice and orange peel into a mixing glass. Add handful of ice cubes and stir until chilled. Strain through a julep strainer over large ice cube in a chilled old-fashioned glass. Pull a long strip of orange peel over the glass, releasing oils into cocktail. Gently pinch, peel side out, misting oils over surface of the drink. Rub peel around the outside rim of the glass, then add.
Makes 1 drink

BOTTLE BASICS

Glenora Distillery in Cape Breton produced the first single malt whisky made in Canada. We love this well-balanced Scotch for its nutty, spicy and honey flavours.

HOT BUTTERED RUM

This riff on the classic Hot Buttered Rum is brightened by the use of a compound butter that blends salted butter and bakeapple. If you can't get your hands on bakeapple, plain butter (instead of the compound butter) will do the trick.

4 cups apple cider, preferably unsweetened
12 oz Newfoundland Screech Rum or dark rum
4 tsp chilled Bakeapple Compound Butter or
    4 tsp chilled salted butter + 1 Tbsp honey
6 cinnamon sticks, for garnish (optional)

Pour cider into a large saucepan. Set over medium heat. Heat until steaming but not boiling. If cider is very sweet, dilute with a bit of water.

Set out 6 warmed heatproof mugs or Irish coffee glasses. Pour 2 oz screech into each mug. If using compound butter, omit honey. If using regular butter, spoon ½ tsp honey into each mug. Pour ⅔ cup warm cider into each mug. Thinly slice compound or regular butter. Top each drink with a little butter. Garnish with cinnamon sticks, if you like.
Makes 6 drinks

> *Bakeapple Compound Butter* <

In a small bowl, stir 1 Tbsp room-temperature butter, preferably lightly salted, with 1 tsp bakeapple or apple jelly. Mound on top of plastic wrap and roll into a small log. Wrap and refrigerate until chilled. Compound butter will keep, sealed and refrigerated, for up to 2 weeks. Makes 4 tsp

MAKING ADJUSTMENTS
This recipe is easily divided or multiplied to suit your guest list.

WARMING TIP
Prepare just like you would for a cup of tea: fill heatproof mugs with boiling water and let stand until cocktail is ready.

Hot & Cold BUTTERED RUMS

COLD BUTTERED RUM

Buttered Rums aren't just reserved for winter anymore. We used rich and caramel-ized apple butter in place of the usual warm apple cider topped with butter. The result is a refreshing, summer-suited sparkling twist.

1 ½ oz spiced rum, such as Lamb's Palm Breeze
1 Tbsp apple butter
¼ oz Spiced Cinnamon Syrup (page 182)
¼ oz freshly squeezed lemon juice
2 dashes Angostura bitters
Handful of ice cubes
2 oz chilled club soda

Pour all ingredients except ice and soda into a cocktail shaker. Add ice and shake until chilled. Double strain through a Hawthorne strainer and a fine-mesh strainer into a measuring cup with a spout. If needed, use the back of a spoon to gently press some of the solids through the sieve. Pour into a chilled coupe glass. Add soda. Gently stir to mix.
Makes 1 drink

Apple Butter

The name's a little misleading, as there's no dairy in apple butter, but this concentrated apple sauce does have a spreadable quality similar to that of butter. Look out for it at your local farmers' market.

LABRADOR ICED TEA

This take on a classic Long Island Iced Tea features Labrador tea leaf, a wild edible native to most of Canada and found even in the far north of Labrador. We use the leaves for both an infusion and a chilled tea. Mixed together, they result in a powerful, refreshing drink that's fit for a group.

2 oz freshly squeezed lemon juice
2 oz white rum
2 oz blanco tequila
2 oz gin
2 oz vodka
2 oz orange liqueur, such as Cointreau
1 ½ oz Simple Syrup (page 182)
2 Tbsp dried Labrador tea leaves,
  coarsely broken if needed
2-cup jar with new lid and ring, sterilized
1 cup Chilled Labrador Tea
Large handful of ice cubes

Pour all ingredients except Chilled Labrador Tea and ice into the jar and seal tightly. Shake vigorously. Refrigerate, shaking once an hour, for 3 hours. Strain through a funnel lined with several layers of cheesecloth into a teapot. Just before serving, add Chilled Labrador Tea and ice to teapot. Serve in 6 oz teacups over 1 to 2 ice cubes.

Makes 4 drinks

> Chilled Labrador Tea <

Bring 1 cup water to a boil over high heat. Remove from heat. Once water stops boiling, add 1 Tbsp dried Labrador tea leaves. Let infuse, sealed, for 2 hours. Fine strain into a resealable container. Refrigerate until chilled, about 1 hour. Makes 8 oz (1 cup)

Labrador Tea (Ledum groenlanicum)

This wild edible, also known as Hudson's Bay tea or bog tea, is an evergreen shrub. The dried leaves, which are green on top and reddish and fuzzy underneath, are usually used for a soothing warm tea. You may find references to Labrador tea toxicity, but we drink it all the time with no ill effects. Also, Alexander Cruz of Société-Orignal dispels this notion by saying that to experience toxic effects, "you would need to consume pounds and pounds of it in a single sitting." You can order it from them or D'Origina Être Boréal.

ST. JOHN'S SLING

This riff on a Singapore Sling #2 subs in Newfoundland screech in place of gin and showcases cloudberry liqueur instead of the usual grenadine. The bar requirements for this drink are a bit hefty, but you can put them to use in classic cocktails, as well as in many of the other cocktails in this book.

1 ½ oz unsweetened pineapple juice
1 ½ oz Newfoundland Screech Rum
1 oz freshly squeezed orange juice
½ oz freshly squeezed lemon juice
½ oz cloudberry liqueur, such as
      Rodrigues, Chicoutai or Lapponia
½ oz Aperol (optional)
¼ oz orange liqueur, such as Cointreau
¼ oz Benedictine
1 dash Angostura bitters
1 dash orange bitters
Large handful of ice cubes
Crushed ice

1 oz chilled club soda
Whole nutmeg, for garnish
Ground cherry (physalis), for garnish

Pour all ingredients except ice, soda and garnishes into a cocktail shaker. Add ice cubes. Double strain through a Hawthorne strainer and a fine-mesh strainer into a chilled collins glass filled with crushed ice. Top with soda. Grate a pinch of nutmeg overtop. Twist leaves of ground cherry together and set overtop.
Makes 1 drink

Cloudberry 101

This delicate golden-tinged berry (also known as bakeapple) grows in Arctic, Subarctic and northern moorland regions, including that of North America. This fruit is used in a variety of confections, as well as in a sweet-fruit, almost-honey-tasting liqueur (used in this recipe). If you're in St. John's, be sure to pick up some bakeapple jam and cloudberry liqueur—they're local specialties.

THE 52%

At the scenic Fogo Island Inn, JACOB LUKSIC makes drinks while icebergs float by in the breathtaking background. A bit of worthwhile prep goes into this locally-sourced cocktail named for the 52% of Newfoundlanders who voted for Confederation in 1948.

2 oz Earl Grey–Infused Rum
¾ oz Ginger Beer Syrup
¾ oz Wild Blueberry Shrub
¾ oz or 1 small egg white
Large handful of ice cubes
1 large ice cube
2 wild blueberries, for garnish

Pour all ingredients except ice and garnish into a cocktail shaker. Dry shake until incorporated and frothy. Add handful of ice cubes and shake until chilled. Double strain through a Hawthorne strainer and a fine-mesh strainer over large ice cube in a chilled old-fashioned glass. When egg foam settles, float blueberries on surface.
Makes 1 drink

> *Earl Grey–Infused Rum* <

Add 3 cups white rum and ¼ cup Earl Grey tea leaves to a sterilized jar. Seal. Shake for 15 seconds. Infuse for 2 to 4 hours. Strain through a funnel lined with a coffee filter or several layers of cheese-cloth. Will keep well for at least 3 months. Makes about 24 oz (3 cups), for 12 drinks

> *Ginger Beer Syrup* <

Pour 2 ¼ cups good-quality ginger beer into a small saucepan. Boil until reduced by half, 20 to 22 minutes. Cool completely. Will keep, sealed in a jar and refrigerated, for 2 weeks. Makes 9 oz (1 cup + 2 Tbsp), for 13 drinks

> *Wild Blueberry Shrub* <

Place 2 cups wild blueberries in a jar. Lightly muddle. Add 1 cup apple cider vinegar. Seal. Shake, several times a day, for 4 days. Strain vinegar through a fine-mesh strainer lined with cheesecloth into a small saucepan. Bring to a gentle boil. Add 1 cup brown sugar, stirring until dissolved. Cool completely. Shrub will keep, sealed in a jar and refrigerated, for 2 weeks. Makes 12 oz (1 ½ cups), for 17 drinks

NAN'S KITCHEN

Owner of one of Canada's most fun and extensive cocktail supply stores, BYOB Cocktail Emporium (in Toronto), KRISTEN VOISEY hails from Newfoundland. Kristen's play on the Painkiller cocktail uses Newfoundland staples such as partridgeberry jelly, evaporated milk, canned pineapple juice and Lamb's rum—all items commonly found in a Newfoundland nan's kitchen. She also calls for iceberg ice, a cherished provincial ingredient, and instructs to "listen to the ancient ice bubbles crackle."

2 oz Lamb's Palm Breeze Rum
1 oz partridgeberry jelly
1 oz canned pineapple juice
1 oz orange juice
1 oz Carnation evaporated milk
3 dashes Angostura bitters
1 dash Grand Marnier
Handful of ice cubes
Hunk of iceberg ice or 1 large ice cube
1 thick orange peel strip, for garnish

Pour all ingredients except ice and garnish into a cocktail shaker, using a dropper to add a dash of Grand Marnier. Add handful of ice cubes. Shake until chilled. Pour over a hunk of iceberg ice in an old-fashioned glass. Garnish by fastening orange peel to the glass using a small clothespin.

SHOPPING TIP

Many of the beautiful glasses, tools and accessories featured within the pages of this book are available at BYOB Cocktail Emporium.

The NORTH

RECIPES IN THIS SECTION:

YUKON GOLD RUSH

ARCTIC MARTINEZ

THE BUSH PILOT

THE SPELL OF THE YUKON

THE YUKON SOURTOE SHOT

The northern territories are truly North America's final frontier. Combined, Yukon, Northwest Territories and Nunavut cover nearly four million square kilometres and claim some of the world's most beautiful natural wonders. Yukon is home to Mount Logan, Canada's highest peak. The Northwest Territories have many of the country's most spectacular waterfalls, including Virginia Falls, which are twice as tall as Niagara Falls. Where better to experience the magic of the aurora borealis than on the Arctic islands of Nunavut? As Yukon-born-and-raised writer Pierre Berton describes in *Why We Act Like Canadians*, "Few have seen the cliffs of Baffin or the eskers of the tundra but we all live cheek by jowl with the wilderness; and all of us, I think, feel the empty and awesome presence of the North . . . an uncanny environment that beckons even as it repels, seductive in its beauty, fearsome in its splendor." Many artists are drawn northward, seeking to capture and instill its majestic, mysterious beauty in any way possible, and we would like to extend that endeavour to a good cocktail. We look to past stories of hard-core northern spirit, celebrating local heroes like poet Robert Service (see page 177). We also highlight wild homegrown flavours and take inspiration from the scenery and edible bounty, as with our Arctic Martinez (page 175).

The North has no shortage of awe-inspiring scenery, but with much of the population in remote areas and many communities still deeply steeped in tradition, it's not exactly cocktail country. Having hitchhiked years ago from Prince George up the Alaska highway to Yukon, Scott can say with confidence that the cocktail scene is mostly concentrated in the more heavily populated cities. He did find, however, that keeping a good bottle of whisky on you as you journey north can certainly help a traveller make friends. He also found that there are great places to enjoy a good drink and that there is growing support for local brewing and distilling, particularly in the major cities. Whitehorse is home to Yukon Brewing, which makes great beer, and to its sister company, Yukon Spirits, which invents creative distilling experiments, such as beer schnapps and berry marc. Whitehorse is also home to Yukon Shine Distillery, whose bottles are hitting shelves across the country. In Dawson City, a remnant of the Klondike days with a strong summer tourism industry, pubs like Bombay Peggy's, housed in Yukon's only restored brothel-turned-inn, serve mixed drinks with cheeky, taboo titles. Diamond Tooth Gerties Gambling Hall is a

Klondike-themed entertainment hot spot with a casino and nightly cancan shows. And, of course, you can't miss the Sourdough Saloon in the Downtown Hotel, where you can join the more than 50,000 people who have sampled the infamous Sourtoe Cocktail, a baffling tradition involving a severed human toe (which we pay tribute to on page 178). Even though Scott is a certified member of the Sourtoe Cocktail Club, having properly kissed the appendage, we opted to swap out the dehydrated digit for something more appealing.

The Sourtoe Cocktail is only one example of the hard-core spirit that thrives in the North. Survival in the harsh Arctic and Subarctic is no joke, and yet communities and cities there not only survive but continue to grow. Yukon owes much of its growth to the Klondike gold rush of the 1890s, which had upward of 100,000 people making the trek northward. It's a long, arduous journey, and more than half didn't make it, either returning home or suffering worse fates. Dawson City was the main destination for prospectors and at one point was the biggest city west of Winnipeg and north of Seattle, with over 30,000 residents. The Yukon Gold Rush (page 173) is our way of recognizing the times and people who paved the way to building up the territory we know today. Well, with the North being so

remote, paving isn't really a proper metaphor. There is only one paved road in all of Nunavut—in its capital, Iqaluit, which is otherwise not connected by roads to the rest of Canada. This isolation makes it difficult for inhabitants there to get the latest and greatest products available in cities and bars farther south. In Nunavut, which still practises Prohibition in some parts, alcohol orders are shipped almost entirely by air cargo. This practice began when Canada started using planes for mail carriage, roughly around the 1920s, and naturally, liquor was a common care package. The very first test of air-mail carriage was in 1918 when Captain Brian Peck flew from Montreal to Toronto with a load of cargo. Since Prohibition was by then over, he decided to transport booze—so much so that the plane could not fly more than twelve metres off the ground. Canada's North, once inaccessible in winter without use of dog sleds, owes much of its growth and history to the aviators who helped create a connection between it and the rest of the country. In the days after World War I, planes were used to establish settlements, landing strips and highway routes, and also to transport engineers and provide them with the materials and sustenance needed for research and development. Yellowknife recognizes its bush pilots as heroes and has dedicated a monument to them in Old Town. We devote a cocktail to the aviators who played such an integral role in opening up the North (see page 176).

Like the artists and bush pilots who braved the cold to blaze new trails, we also hope to carve out new territory, this time with a few drinks, each inspired by one of the most unexplored places on earth. It will be hard not to notice that we have significantly fewer recipes dedicated to these parts, but since northerners are adventurers and innovators, we will be watching cocktail culture in the North closely, and in the meantime, we've infused some of that unyielding spirit into this collection of creative drinks that represent this matchless and fascinating region of Canada.

YUKON GOLD RUSH

We couldn't resist both the allure and the challenge of combining the black sheep of Canadian liqueurs, Yukon Jack (not easy to mix or even drink straight) with the beauty of a Gold Rush. We fell in love with the modern classic after trying out the recipe originally developed by T.J. Siegel, featured in the *PDT Cocktail Book*. Our take also includes mildly floral fireweed honey to celebrate a local treat and the official flower of Yukon.

1 ½ oz bourbon
¾ oz Yukon Jack Liqueur
¾ oz Honey Syrup (page 183), preferably using fireweed honey
¾ oz freshly squeezed lemon juice
Large handful of ice cubes
1 lemon peel strip

Pour all ingredients except ice and lemon peel into a cocktail shaker. Add ice and shake until chilled. Double strain through a Hawthorne strainer and a fine-mesh strainer into a chilled coupe glass. Using a peeler, pull a long strip of lemon peel over the glass, releasing oils into cocktail. Gently pinch, peel side out, misting oils over surface of the drink. Rub peel around the outside rim of the glass, then discard peel.
Makes 1 drink

Fireweed

This bright pink flower can be found in dry mountainous regions and spreads into open areas, including forest-fire scorched ones. If you can't get your hands on fireweed honey, use a local wildflower honey in its place.

ARCTIC MARTINEZ

This northern twist on a classic Martinez uses an Arctic rose vermouth reduction, which has a beautiful pale pink hue reminiscent of a sunset over Arctic snow. The delicate Arctic rose (also known as the prickly wild rose) is a species that grows wild in almost every Canadian province and into the northern territories. Feel free to use any edible rose.

2 oz Arctic Rose Vermouth Reduction
1 oz gin, such as Yukon Shine Distillery AuraGin
1 tsp Aperol
Handful of ice cubes
1 edible dried rose petal, preferably Arctic rose,
　　for garnish

Pour all ingredients except ice and garnish into a mixing glass. Add ice and stir until chilled. Strain through a julep strainer into a chilled coupe glass. Garnish with rose petal.
Makes 1 drink

> *Arctic Rose Vermouth Reduction* <

Place 4 cups white sweet vermouth and 12 edible dried rose buds, preferably Arctic rose, in a large saucepan. Set over high heat and bring to a boil. Reduce heat to medium. Gently boil until reduced to exactly 2 cups including roses, about 45 minutes. Remove from heat and let cool completely. Fine strain through a funnel lined with several layers of cheesecloth. Reduction will keep, sealed and refrigerated, for 1 month. Makes 14 oz (1 ¾ cups), for 7 drinks

THE BUSH PILOT

This spirit-forward cocktail is our toast to the northern pilots. We took some basics from a classic Aviation cocktail, given its complementary nature and name. Our spirit-forward number uses birch syrup—a northern delicacy—and the fantastic Amaro Montenegro bitter liqueur. Look for birch syrup in specialty shops or buy online. (See drink photo on page 33.)

1 ½ oz gin, such as Yukon Shine Distillery
   AuraGin
¾ oz Amaro Montenegro
½ oz freshly squeezed lemon juice
½ tsp maraschino liqueur
¼ tsp birch syrup
Large handful of ice cubes
1 homemade cocktail cherry (page 188)
   or store-bought, for garnish

Pour all ingredients except ice and garnish into a cocktail shaker. Add ice and shake until chilled. Double strain through a Hawthorne strainer and a fine-mesh strainer into a chilled coupe glass. Garnish with cherry.

Makes 1 drink

Birch Syrup

The taste of this syrup can be quite polarizing.
Its incredibly unique flavour isn't a substitute for its
more popular cousin, maple syrup. Instead, put it to use
in cooking or sparingly in cocktails—a little goes a long way.

THE SPELL OF THE YUKON

We hope you fall under the spell of this cocktail, which may remind you of the surprising effect of the land that Robert Service describes in "The Spell of the Yukon," from *Songs of a Sourdough*, which inspired this captivating springtime delight. Rhubarb is cherished in the North because it manages to grow in the challenging climate. When it's in season, it can be found at markets such as the Fireweed Community Market in Whitehorse, grocery stores and even at some gas stations.

1 ½ oz Rhubarb-Infused Pisco
¾ oz freshly squeezed lime juice
¾ oz Simple Syrup (page 182)
2 dashes orange bitters
Large handful of ice cubes
Splash chilled club soda
Rhubarb ribbon, for garnish (optional)

Pour all ingredients except ice, soda and garnish into a cocktail shaker. Add ice and shake until chilled. Double strain through a Hawthorne strainer and a fine-mesh strainer into a chilled coupe glass. Top with soda. Garnish with rhubarb ribbon.

Makes 1 drink

> *Rhubarb-Infused Pisco* <

Pour 1 cup chopped fresh or frozen rhubarb into a sterilized resealable jar. Pour 1 cup pisco overtop. Shake and let stand until flavour infuses and colour has been fully extracted, 2 to 7 days. Fine strain through a coffee filter–lined funnel into a sterilized resealable jar. Infused pisco will keep in a cool, dark place for at least 3 months. Makes scant 8 oz (1 cup) for 5 drinks

---

Songs of a Sourdough

Robert Service, the Bard of the Yukon, may be most famous for his poems "The Cremation of Sam McGee" and "The Shooting of Dan McGrew," which can be found in his 1907 compilation *Songs of a Sourdough*, along with the poem that inspired this drink.

THE YUKON SOURTOE SHOT

Here is our ode to the infamous Sourtoe Cocktail, available at the Sourdough Saloon in Dawson City. We opt for a morel mushroom—a Yukon favourite that's plentiful up north—in place of a human toe. Think of it as an edible pickleback (the practice of chasing whisky with a little pickle brine).

1 Pickled Morel Mushroom

1 oz whisky, such as Wiser's Small Batch, Proof Whisky, Jameson Irish Whiskey or Yukon Jack Liqueur

Skewer pickled morel. Set over whisky-filled shot glass. Shoot, then chew.

Makes 1 drink

> *Pickled Morel Mushrooms* <

Gently brush off any dirt from 1 cup or 2 oz fresh morel mushrooms. Cut into bite-sized pieces—quarters or halves, depending on size. Fill the sink or a large bowl with cold water. Add a generous amount of coarse kosher salt, stirring to dissolve it. Add mushrooms and let stand for 10 to 20 minutes, gently stirring occasionally. Using a slotted spoon, transfer mushrooms to a strainer. Morels have a tendency to carry undesirable travellers; if there are any, the salt will draw them out. Repeat the saltwater rinse process until nothing lingers at the bottom of the sink. Thoroughly rinse soaked morels. Drain off excess liquid. Scatter mushrooms on paper towels and let stand until fairly dry.

Set a medium-sized skillet over medium heat. Add 1 Tbsp butter, preferably unsalted. When bubbling, turn pan to coat, then add mushrooms. Cook, stirring occasionally, until softened, 3 to 5 minutes. Spoon into a sterilized jar. Place 1/3 cup white wine vinegar, 1/3 cup water, 3/4 tsp coarse kosher salt, 1/2 tsp whole black peppercorns, 1/4 tsp coriander seeds, 1/4 tsp granulated sugar in a small saucepan. Set over medium heat. Heat until steaming but not boiling, stirring to help dissolve salt and sugar. Pour over mushrooms, leaving 1/2 inch headspace in jar. Seal tightly with lid and ring. Refrigerate. When butter has risen to the surface and is firm, skim off and discard. Pickled mushrooms will keep, sealed and refrigerated, for at least 1 week. Makes 8 oz (1 cup)

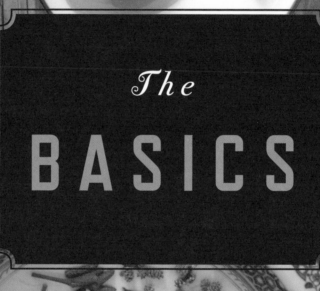

The
BASICS

Preparing homemade versions of the ingredients that go into cocktails can have astonishing results. Here are our recipes for the basics, so you can make your own simple syrups, tonic syrup, cocktail cherries, cordial and more. Aside from using these handcrafted recipes when called for in our book, try them in classic cocktails and your own creative drinks too.

IN THIS SECTION

SYRUP 101

SIMPLE SYRUP

SIMPLE SYRUP VARIATIONS

INFUSION 101

INFUSIONS

TONIC

CANADIAN COCKTAIL CHERRIES

BLACKBERRY GRENADINE

TRADITIONAL-STYLE GRENADINE

RASPBERRY CORDIAL

BLACK WALNUT ORGEAT

TOMATO-CLAM JUICE

SYRUP 101

Simple syrup is included as a sweetener in many traditional cocktail recipes. It's easy to put your own spin on it. You'll find several of our variations below.

> *Simple Syrup* <

This recipe can work in any amount you like as long as equal parts are used. So double, triple or quadruple it; just keep in mind that the sugar may take a minute or two longer to dissolve. Store syrup (or variations) in a sterilized jar sealed with a new lid and ring. Each will keep, refrigerated, for at least 2 weeks and sometimes up to 1 month.

Stir 1 cup granulated sugar with 1 cup water in a small saucepan. Set over medium heat. Stir occasionally until sugar is dissolved, about 5 minutes. Makes 12 oz (1½ cups)

> *Ginger Syrup* <

Wash 1 unpeeled piece ginger, about 6 inches long or 3.5 oz. Cut into ¼-inch slices. Stir 1 cup granulated sugar and ginger with 1 cup water in a small saucepan. Set over medium heat. Bring to a gentle boil, stirring occasionally and gently pressing on ginger. Remove from heat and let cool completely. Fine strain through a funnel lined with a coffee filter or several layers of cheesecloth. Makes 10 oz (1 ¼ cups)

> *Cinnamon Syrup* <

Place 1 cup granulated sugar, 1 cup water and 3 cinnamon sticks in a small saucepan. Set over medium heat. Bring to a simmer. Remove from heat and let cool completely. Fine strain through a funnel lined with several layers of cheesecloth. Makes 12 oz (1 ½ cups)

> *Spiced Cinnamon Syrup* <

Stir ½ cup granulated sugar with ½ cup water in a small saucepan. Add 1 cinnamon stick, 5 whole cloves and ½ tsp freshly grated lime zest. Set over medium heat. Stir occasionally until sugar is dissolved, about 5 minutes. Remove from heat and let cool completely. Fine strain through a funnel lined with a coffee filter or several layers of cheesecloth. Makes 6 oz (¾ cup)

> *Balsam Fir Syrup* <

Place 1 cup granulated sugar, 1 cup water and 5 balsam fir tips in a small saucepan. Set over medium heat. Bring just to a simmer. Remove from heat and let cool completely. Fine strain through a funnel lined with several layers of cheesecloth. Makes 12 oz (1 ½ cups)

> *Rhubarb-Peppercorn Syrup* <

Place 3 thickly sliced trimmed rhubarb stalks, 1 cup granulated sugar, 1 cup water and 15 white peppercorns in a small saucepan. Set over medium heat. Gently simmer until rhubarb is very tender. Remove from heat and let cool completely. Using the back of a ladle, swirl and push through a sieve into a sterilized jar. (Keep the rhubarb purée that's left behind for another use, such as spreading on toast.) Makes 10 to 12 oz (1 ¼ to 1 ½ cups)

> *Rich Syrup* <

Place 1 cup granulated sugar and ½ cup water in a small saucepan. Set over medium heat. Stir occasionally until sugar is dissolved, about 5 minutes. Makes 8 oz (1 cup)

> *Rich Blueberry Syrup* <

Place 2 cups granulated sugar, 1 cup water and ½ cup fresh blueberries in a small saucepan. Set over medium heat. Stir occasionally until mixture reaches a gentle simmer. Remove from heat. Using a wooden spoon, mash and press on blueberries to release juices. Stir, then let cool completely. Fine strain through a funnel lined with several layers of cheesecloth. Repeat if needed. Makes 12 oz (1 ½ cups)

> *Honey Syrup* <

Place 1 Tbsp honey in a small bowl. Add 1 Tbsp hot water. Stir until honey is dissolved. If making more than one cocktail, multiply honey syrup accordingly. If needed, gently heat mixture in a small saucepan until honey is dissolved. Let cool completely. To make a rich honey syrup, double the honey, keeping the water the same. Makes 1 oz (2 Tbsp)

INFUSION 101

This simple cocktail technique is a great way to draw out and preserve the flavours from your favourite ingredients—everything from herbs and spices to citrus and berries. We've had great results incorporating tea, dried flowers and herbs, spices, vegetables, fruits and even butter. The key is to taste and adjust as you like before straining. Ingredient potency and alcohol flavours yield varying results, so experiment. Liqueurs and alcohol-based infusions will keep, sealed and stored in a cool, dark place, for at least 3 months.

> *Lavender-Infused Gin* <

Pour 1 cup gin into sterilized jar. Add ¾ tsp dried lavender buds. Shake, then let stand to infuse for 6 hours. Fine strain through a coffee filter–lined funnel into a sterilized jar. Makes 8 oz (1 cup)

> *Seamist Tea–Infused Vodka* <

Pour 1 cup Victoria Spirits Left Coast Hemp Vodka into sterilized jar. Add 2 tsp Silk Road Tea's Seamist tea leaves or mint tea leaves. Shake, then let stand to infuse for 12 minutes. Fine strain through a coffee filter–lined funnel into a sterilized jar. Makes 8 oz (1 cup)

> Brown Butter–Infused Unaged Whisky <

Place ¼ cup butter into a small skillet. Set over medium heat. Cook, swirling pan occasionally, until butter is amber coloured, 5 to 7 minutes. Immediately pour into a 2-cup sterilized jar. Pour in 1 cup unaged whisky. Seal and let stand for 3 hours. Refrigerate for 1 to 3 days. Remove from fridge and skim fat from top. Strain through a funnel lined with several layers of cheesecloth into a 2-cup sterilized jar. Seal with a new lid and ring. Will keep on your bar shelf for at least 1 month. Makes 7 ½ oz

---

> Pine-Infused Canadian Whisky <

Place 3 Tbsp snipped or coarsely chopped washed regular pine needles, white pine needles or white pine tea leaves in a Mason jar. Pour 1 cup Canadian whisky, such as Wiser's or Canadian Club, overtop. Seal and shake. Let stand until flavours infuse but do not overpower, about 3 hours. Strain through a coffee filter-lined funnel into sterilized jar. Makes 8 oz (1 cup)

SAFE STORAGE

When making syrups, infusions and liqueurs, it's important to fine strain thoroughly to remove solid particles, which could contribute to spoilage. Whenever possible, use a very fine filter such as a coffee filter or wine filter (often found at wine supply stores). Some sedimentation may occur, but is not always troublesome. Sediment will normally rest at the bottom of the jar. Bacteria isn't always visible, but some signs that can indicate your recipe is past its prime are particles floating near the surface or anything cloudy and billowy within. It's not always possible to see either of these clearly, so be sure to follow the recommended guidelines for safe storage.

TONIC

Making your own tonic syrup is easier than you think and it will dramatically improve your next G&T. The hardest part is getting the cinchona (see tip below). The flavour of homemade tonic is worth the effort. And once you've tucked away this homemade syrup in your fridge, all you'll need is sparkling or carbonated water to make it a bubbly soda tonic.

1 grapefruit
1 lemon
1 lime
1 to 2 lemongrass stalks
2 cups granulated sugar
2 cups water
1 Tbsp cinchona bark (not powdered)
Small pinch coarse kosher salt
7 white peppercorns (optional)

Finely grate zest from grapefruit, lemon and lime, measuring out 1 tsp of each. Trim lemongrass and peel, if needed, then coarsely chop. Measure out 3 Tbsp. Place sugar and water into a medium saucepan. Set over medium heat. Stir occasionally until sugar is dissolved, 5 to 7 minutes. Stir in all remaining ingredients, including citrus zests. Continue cooking, stirring occasionally, for 5 minutes. Adjust heat so mixture gently heats or almost simmers but does not boil. Remove from heat. Cover and let infuse for 10 minutes. Uncover and let stand until cool, allowing flavours to infuse. When completely cool, strain through a fine-mesh strainer. Then fine strain through a funnel lined with a coffee filter or several layers of cheesecloth.
Makes 22 to 24 oz (2 ¾ to 3 cups)

CINCHONA
This bark can be bought in small chunks or powdered form. This bittering agent is not your everyday ingredient but is essential in making traditional tonic syrup. Look for it at your local herbal supply, or bulk store, or order it online.

CANADIAN COCKTAIL CHERRIES

Making your own boozy cherries is easier than you might think. The results are tasty, naturally coloured sweet or tart cherries infused with your bottle of choice.

2 cups pitted sour Morello or sweet
    Bing cherries
¼ vanilla bean
½ cup granulated sugar
¼ cup water
1 cinnamon stick
1 whole clove
1 lemon or orange peel strip
2-cup jar with new lid and ring, sterilized
½ cup brandy, kirsch, rye whisky,
    maple eau-de-vie or maraschino liqueur

Pit cherries. Carefully cut a small slit down side of vanilla bean with a paring knife. Use the blunt side of the knife to scrape out seeds. Place seeds and pod in a small saucepan along with sugar, water, cinnamon, clove and lemon peel. Gently heat over medium-low heat, stirring occasionally, until sugar is dissolved, about 5 minutes. Fine strain. Pour back into saucepan. Add cherries. Gently heat, stirring occasionally and without simmering, until softened slightly, about 3 minutes. Let cool slightly. Using a slotted spoon, carefully spoon cherries into jar. Add liqueur to syrup, stirring to combine. Pour over cherries. Wipe rim with a clean, damp cloth. Seal jar with lid and ring. Let cool completely. Cherries will keep, sealed and refrigerated, for up to 3 months.
Makes 16 oz (2 cups)

Mix It Up

We love the result of mixing spirits in this recipe.
For example, we had great results using
1 ½ oz each whisky, kirsch and brandy.

BLACKBERRY GRENADINE

This recipe yields a thick and velvety grenadine. The fresh blackberry flavour really shines through. The key is to use sweet blackberries and to avoid overly tart or sour ones; otherwise, the grenadine will carry the same flavour.

4 cups fresh blackberries
½ cup Simple Syrup (page 182)
1 oz vodka

Using a juicer, extract juice from blackberries. Or whirl blackberries in a food processor until puréed, then strain through a fine-mesh sieve into a large bowl and use a ladle to swirl and press to extract juices. Pour juice into a large measuring cup. You should have about 1 ½ cups. Stir in simple syrup and vodka. Grenadine will keep well, sealed and refrigerated, for up to 1 week. Grenadine may separate as it sits, so shake before using.

Makes 16 oz (2 cups)

TRADITIONAL-STYLE GRENADINE

2 large or 3 small pomegranates
6 oz Simple Syrup (page 182)
1 oz vodka

Seed pomegranate and extract juice. Whirl 3 cups seeds in a food processor. Fine strain through a fine-mesh sieve into a large measuring cup. Use a ladle to swirl and press to extract any excess juices. You should have about 1 ½ cups. Stir in simple syrup and vodka. Transfer to jar. Grenadine will keep, sealed and refrigerated, for at least 1 week.

Makes 18 oz (2 ¼ cups)

SEEDING POMEGRANATES

Slice and crack open pomegranate. Remove seeds to a bowl. Pour cold water overtop. Scoop out and discard pith as it floats to the top. Drain seeds, then pat dry with paper towels.

RASPBERRY CORDIAL

This liqueur is ridiculously easy to make and an excellent way to preserve flavours from your favourite seasonal produce. Essentially, three ingredients and a little patience are all you need. The deep flavours of raspberries work perfectly in cordial form and make a lovely after-dinner digestif.

3 cups fresh raspberries (approximately 12 oz)
4-cup jar with new lid and ring, sterilized
½ cup granulated sugar
2 cups vodka

Gently rinse raspberries. Dry by scattering on paper towels. Add raspberries to jar. Pour sugar overtop. Pour in vodka. Seal tightly with lid and ring. Shake. Store in a cool, dark place until flavours infuse, at least 1 month. Flavour will continue to deepen, and benefits from even longer infusion times, such as 2 to 3 months. Shake every few days. When flavour is infused, strain through a coffee filter–lined funnel into a large measuring cup with a spout. Rinse jar, then pour cordial back in. Cordial will keep, sealed and stored in a cool, dark place, for at least 3 months.
Makes 22 oz (2 ¾ cups)

RASPBERRY CORDIAL
PREPARATION

REGULAR WALNUTS
AND BLACK
WALNUTS FOR
ORGEAT

INFUSION PREPARATION
WITH LABRADOR TEA LEAVES

POMEGRANATE
AND BLACKBERRIES
FOR GRENADINE

BLACK WALNUT ORGEAT

Traditionally, orgeat is an almond-based syrup that's smooth and milky with a hint of floral. It works well in cocktails, lending lots of nutty flavour and silky texture. This homemade version is made with walnuts, black ones if you come across them. It's a thicker incarnation that has intense flavour. Give it a shake before using, as it may separate as it sits.

½ lb fresh black or regular walnuts
2 cups cold water, divided
¾ cup demerara sugar
¼ oz Canadian rye whisky
¼ tsp orange blossom water
2-cup jar with new lid and ring, sterilized

Place nuts in a bowl. Pour in water. Soak for 1 hour. Whirl in a food processor until almost finely ground. Strain through a fine-mesh sieve. Gently press with the back of a wooden spoon to extract excess liquids. This first liquid is quite bitter, so discard it. Place ground nuts in bowl. Pour 1 cup water overtop. Let stand loosely covered for 2 to 3 hours. Strain through a sieve lined with several layers of cheesecloth into a large bowl, reserving liquid. When most of liquid is strained, create a bundle with the cheesecloth and squeeze, extracting any excess liquid. The liquid should measure about 1 ¼ cups in total. Pour into a saucepan and stir in sugar. Set over medium heat. Stirring occasionally, heat (but do not allow mixture to boil) until sugar is dissolved, 3 to 5 minutes. Remove from heat and let cool completely. Stir in whisky and orange blossom water. Refrigerate until chilled. Orgeat will keep, sealed and refrigerated, for up to 3 weeks. Shake before using.

Makes 14 oz (1 ¾ cups)

A Tough Nut to Crack

Black walnut is well known for putting down roots in Central Canada. When it comes to getting to the heart of a walnut, spread it on an old kitchen towel, cover with another kitchen towel, then gently hammer the shell to crack it open. Or buy packaged shelled walnuts—this way you'll also avoid stains: black walnut hulls are used to make dye.

TOMATO-CLAM JUICE

Use up the abundance of summer garden tomatoes by making homemade Tomato-Clam Juice. It's a great way to perfect the spices to your liking.

2 very large Great White or 6 medium
    red tomatoes
1 sprig fresh lovage or 1 celery rib
3 Tbsp store-bought clam juice or leftover
    broth from steaming clams (be careful to
    not include any sand)
1 tsp freshly squeezed lemon juice
Dashes hot sauce
Pinches salt, freshly ground black pepper
    and granulated sugar

Core tomatoes. In a food processor, pulse until coarsely chopped. You should have 2 ¾ to 3 cups. Pour into a medium saucepan. Set over medium heat. Simmer, stirring frequently, until thickened slightly, about 6 minutes. Carefully return to food processor. Add lovage and whirl until puréed. Strain through a fine-mesh sieve. Using the back of a spoon or a ladle, push through as much juice as possible. Pour juice into a jar or pitcher. Stir in clam and lemon juices and seasonings. Taste and adjust to your liking. Juice will keep, sealed and refrigerated, for up to 3 days.
Makes 22 oz (2 ¾ cups)

FOOD & COCKTAILS

OYSTER GUIDE

Canada can claim truly remarkable oyster offerings. Each type carries its own unique tastes, which can vary greatly from mollusc to mollusc, even when they're grown in nearby shores. A glass of something fantastic makes an oyster experience complete. Go beyond wine or bubbly and experiment with pairing these beautiful bivalves with a cocktail. Here's our guide to storing, shucking and choosing—and suggestions for cocktail pairings.

STORING Keep oysters unshucked, cup-side down, to preserve their precious and tasty liquor. Arrange them in a bowl over ice and covered with damp paper towels. Tuck them in the back of the fridge, where it's coldest—they'll stay fresh for a couple days.

PREPARING Scrub to clean, loosening and brushing away any dirt or grit. Discard any open or cracked oysters. Before you start shucking, prepare the accompaniments, such as lemon wedges and mignonette (heavy on the shallots).

SHUCKING Protect your hand with a thick kitchen towel or, better yet, use a protective oyster-shucking glove. Secure oysters cup-side down on a kitchen towel. Using the palm of your hand, press the cloth into the top of the shell in the opposite direction of the oyster knife. Slide the knife into the crook of the shell—the tiny opening at the point of the oyster. Carefully shimmy the flat side of the knife between the top and bottom halves of the shell. Twist, prying open the shells, then run the blade along the roof of the shell to release the oyster. As best you can, avoid pushing any shards into the liquor. Repeat with the bottom half, slicing through the oyster adductor and releasing the oyster. Serve oysters in their half shell set on a tray filled with crushed ice, the oysters carefully propped up so the liquor doesn't spill out.

EATING We recommend a slurp and at least a couple of chews for ultimate oyster enjoyment.

West Coast oysters are often creamy, rich and buttery, with sweet, sometimes melon-like qualities. They're often distinguishable by their pretty, lacy shells. Noteworthy types include Kusshi, Fanny Bay and Beach Angel. Enjoy paired with our Butchart Garden Swizzle, Prince Edward Bounty, Chinook Sangria or Golden Boy.

WEST COAST CHEF'S CHOICE

We asked Jonathan Chovancek, executive chef of Vancouver's Café Medina and co-proprietor of Bittered Sling Extracts, to weigh in on the advantages of pairing oysters with cocktails. "Gin is an obvious go-to when pairing oysters, as the soft spice of juniper and coriander helps lift the complexity and minerality from the oysters," he says. "Some of my favourite oysters come from Effingham Inlet, in Barkley Sound, BC. Their soft oceanic minerality, with hints of melon and romaine lettuce, pair nicely with a classic French 75."

East Coast oysters generally have straightforward, clean, crisp and briny sea-like flavours. They're often larger than West Coast types, with harder shells. Favourites include Beausoleil, Black Point, Cascumpec Bay, Colville Bay, Lucky Lime, Pickle Point, Raspberry Point and Shiny Sea.

Sip alongside our East–Meets–West Coast Caesar, or try with a Fiddlehead Martini, Sparkling Watermelon Sipper or The Coupe de Cartier.

SHUCKER'S EAST COAST CHOICE

Rodney's Oyster House catering captain Matt Woo shared his favourite tips for pairing East Coast oysters with cocktails. He says, "East Coast oysters tend to have a more delicate texture and stronger salinity than West Coast oysters. Common tasting notes include mushrooms, celery, lemongrass and watercress." Woo suggests "avoiding sweet cocktails, in favour of classics like a gin or vodka martini. A lemon twist will help balance out the salinity of an oyster, while an olive will enhance it."

CANADIAN CHEESE

To say that we like cheese would be an understatement. Victoria has enjoyed writing about cheese for years, which almost justifies the copious amounts we consume. Aside from everyday snacking, we always offer cheese at a party so naturally we marry our love of fromage with cocktails. Unlike with wine, you can adjust the elements in your cocktails to perfectly pair the two.

PAIRING There's a lot to think about when pairing cheeses, including texture, salinity and overall flavour. Generally, stronger and more pungent cheeses match well with drinks that have a bit of oomph, like dark, bold, spiced and aged spirits. Milder cheeses lend themselves nicely to options with gentle and subtle flavour profiles, such as lighter, effervescent, delicately floral and perfumed spirits. The flavours should complement one another but carry compatible amounts of character so that one doesn't drown out the other.

CHEESE+COCKTAIL These are some of our favourite cheeses, with suggested cocktail matches:

- Monforte Dairy Halloumi, grilled, with The Pearl Punch (page 73)

- Laiterie Charlevoix Le 1608 with our Balsam Blend (page 101)

- Thunder Oak Cheese Farm Gouda with our Lavender-Blueberry Sparkler (page 152)

- Salt Spring Chèvre or Fromagerie Le Détour Grey Owl with our Kir or Arctic Martinez (page 175)

- Fromagerie Médard 14 Arpents or Alexis de Port Neuf La Sauvagine with The Bush Pilot (page 176)

ULTIMATE CHEESE BOARD Select at least three to five cheeses: a firm or hard, a creamy and/or soft and something special, like a washed rind and/or something a bit stronger, like a blue. Round out the platter with charcuterie, nuts and fruits—for instance, slices of saucisson or prosciutto, almonds or pistachios and dried apricots or fresh figs—and serve with bread and crackers. If you're including a selection of crackers and bread, make sure to include a plain classic crusty baguette and thin plain wafer crackers.

RECOMMENDED CANADIAN CHEESES

- Blue Juliette, Salt Spring Cheese, BC

- Tiger Blue, Poplar Grove Cheese, BC

- Comox Brie, Natural Pastures Cheese Company, BC

- Old Grizzly, Sylvan Star Cheese Ltd., AB

- Paradiso and Toscano, Monforte, ON

- Lankaaster, Glengarry Fine Cheese, ON

- Niagara Gold, Upper Canada Cheese Company, ON

- Fresh Cheese curds, Fromagerie Saint-Fidèle, QC

- Le Riopelle de l'Isle and Tomme de Grosse-île, Fromagerie l'Île-aux-Grues, QC

- Laliberté and Louis D'or, Fromagerie du Presbyterie, QC

- Alfred le Fermier, Fromagerie le Fermier, QC

- Clandestin and Magie de Madawaska, Fromagerie Le Detour, QC

- Le Baluchon, Fromagerie F.X. Pichet, QC

- Bleu Bénédictin, Fromagerie Abbaye de Saint-Benoît-du-Lac, QC

- Le Douanier or Raclette, Fritz de Kaiser, QC

- Dragon's Breath Blue, That Dutchman's Farm, NS

- Quark, Foxhill Cheese House, NS

- Avonlea Clothbound Cheddar, Cows Creamery, PE

STORING Cheese keeps best with proper storage. Wrap firm cheese and rind cheeses in waxed paper or plastic wrap; store blue cheese in foil.

A DRINKABLE GARDEN

Our cocktail journey began with our garden. Here's a sneak peek into our backyard and some of the delicious ways we drink the fruits of our labours.

HERBS Fresh herbs are a must, even in the smallest outdoor space. You can also grow many varieties in a pot on a sunny windowsill. We like to incorporate both fresh and dried herbs by infusing them in alcohol, preparing simple syrups and shrubs or simply muddling them or using them as a garnish. Just give them a gentle smack between the palms of your hands before using them as a garnish, to bring out their flavour. Plant the following for endless cocktail possibilities.

CLASSICS
Basil

Cilantro and coriander

Lavender

Lemon balm

Mint

Rosemary

Sage

Tarragon

Thyme

UNUSUAL IMPORTS AND NATIVES

Bee balm — This northern native tastes intensely of pepper and oregano. Muddle it or infuse in a spirit. It's also lovely simply smacked and used as a garnish.

Borage — The taste of this herb can be likened to cucumber and is almost too easy to grow. It's a traditional ingredient in a Pimm's Cup. Try freezing its striking purple flowers in ice cubes or using them as an edible garnish.

Lovage — This herb has an intense celery flavour. Use for a fresh salt rimmer (page 6) or as a garnish. Also add it to stocks and soups.

Wild ginger — A northern native that carries a spicy flavour similar to regular ginger. Use this root in syrups or muddle it in drinks. Or dry the root and finely grate to use in cooking.

Lemon verbena — This delicate herb lives up to its name with its lovely citrus taste. We love it infused into simple syrup, muddled into cocktails or used as a fragrant garnish.

MINT

BORAGE

LEMON VERBENA

LOVAGE

FRUITS AND VEGETABLES If you have the extra outdoor space, you can enjoy a seasonal harvest and skip some trips to the grocery store. Fruits and veggies are surprisingly versatile and worth highlighting in your next party menu, drinks included. Here are some of our favourites:

Apples	Use fresh slices and peels as garnish (see page 7) or steep peels in homemade bitters and infusions.
Berries	Smash, infuse or skewer as garnish.
Cucumbers	Muddle in drinks. We adore tiny Mexican sour gherkins for pickling.
Peppers	Try infusing with spicy ones, or pickle small green ones at the end of the season to garnish cocktails such as a martini, Caesar or Bloody Mary. Sweet or spicy are also fantastic muddled into drinks (see pages 52 and 68).
Tomatoes	Use to make homemade Tomato-Clam Juice (page 193) or pickle green ones at the end of the season.

FLOWERS Growing certain flowers will ensure that you have pollinators and beneficial insects paying your garden a visit; edible ones will add enviable garnishes and character to your cocktails. Here are suggestions for beautifying both your garden and your cocktails.

Herbal flowers	Use flowers from classic herbs in place of the usual leaves and sprigs. Delicate white cilantro flowers make pretty, lacy garnishes; light purple sage flowers add intense floral herbaceous aroma.
Nasturtiums	These edible delights make beautiful garnishes and can add complex peppery notes.
Rose	Use vitamin C–rich rosehips for tea, infusions and syrups, and the fresh or dried petals as garnish.
Geraniums	Candy the leaves of certain edible varieties, such as rose-scented and strawberry, to make beautiful toppers for cocktails and desserts: brush leaves with beaten egg white, then toss in granulated sugar and let dry for a few hours.

*T*O BE CONTINUED . . .

The story doesn't end here. The future of Canadian cocktails is wide open, and we will be showcasing even more drinks online. Visit our ever-growing guide at **canadiancocktail.com**, where you'll find more recipes, videos and news on trends and local talent. You'll also find the buyer's guide on where to purchase ingredients and equipment featured in this book. >

INSPIRATIONS, RESOURCES & RECOMMENDED READING

Aspler, Tony. *Canadian Wineries.*
New York: Firefly Books, 2013.

Berton, Pierre. *Why We Act Like Canadians:
A Personal Exploration of Our National
Character.* Toronto: McClelland & Stewart,
1982.

DeGroff, Dale. *The Essential Cocktail:
The Art of Mixing Perfect Drinks.*
New York: Clarkson Potter, 2008.

De Kergommeaux, Davin. *Canadian Whisky:
The Portable Expert.* Toronto: McClelland
& Stewart, 2012.

Leacock, Stephen. *Wet Wit & Dry Humour:
Distilled from the Pages of Stephen Leacock.*
New York: Dodd, Mead, 1931.

Meehan, Jim. *The PDT Cocktail Book: The
Complete Bartender's Guide from the
Celebrated Speakeasy.* New York: Sterling
Epicure, 2011.

Morgenthaler, Jeffrey. *The Bar Book: Elements
of Cocktail Technique.* San Francisco:
Chronicle Books, 2014.

Parsons, Brad Thomas. *Bitters: A Spirited
History of a Classic Cure-All, with Cocktails,
Recipes, and Formulas.* Berkeley: Ten Speed
Press, 2011.

Peterson, Lee Allen. *A Field Guide to Edible
Wild Plants: Eastern and Central North
America.* Boston: Houghton Mifflin, 1977.

Regan, Gary. *The Joy of Mixology.*
New York: Clarkson Potter, 2003.

Robinson, Geoff and Dorothy.
The Nellie J. Banks. Tyne Valley,
PEI: printed by author, 1993.

Saucier, Ted. *Bottoms Up.* New York:
Greystone Press, 1951.

Service, Robert W. *Songs of a Sourdough.*
Toronto: William Briggs, 1908.

Steinke, Gord. *Mobsters & Rumrunners of
Canada: Crossing the Line.* Edmonton:
Folklore, 2003.

Stewart, Amy. *The Drunken Botanist:
The Plants That Create the World's Great
Drinks.* Chapel Hill, NC: Algonquin
Books, 2013.

Stewart, Anita. *Anita Stewart's Canada: The
Food, the Recipes, the Stories.* Toronto:
HarperCollins, 2008.

Stewart, Hilary. *Drink in the Wild: Teas,
Cordials, Jams and More.* Vancouver:
Douglas & McIntyre, 2002.

Trail, Gayla. *Grow Great Grub: Organic Food
from Small Spaces.* New York: Clarkson
Potter, 2010.

Webb, Margaret. *Apples to Oysters: A Food
Lover's Tour of Canadian Farms.* Toronto:
Penguin Group Canada, 2008.

Wondrich, David. *Imbibe! From Absinthe
Cocktail to Whiskey Smash, a Salute in Stories
and Drinks to "Professor" Jerry Thomas,
Pioneer of the American Bar.* New York:
Perigee Books, 2007.

CONVERSION CHART

CUPS	FLUID OUNCES	TABLE-SPOONS	MILLILITERS
1	8	16	240
3/4	6	12	180
2/3	5	11	160
1/2	4	8	120
1/3	3	5	80
1/4	2	4	30
1/8	1	2	30
1/16	.5	1	15

ACKNOWLEDGEMENTS

Since we began this project a few years ago, much to our delight, we have received unlimited encouragement and support from our family and friends. We dedicate this book to the lot of them.

Our kin! Don and Cathy McCallum, who unquestionably support Scott's wacky creative whims, and Keith, Franco, Neil and Katie, for their encouragement and willingness to try out our early experiments. And for helping stock our bar with bottles from all over the world!

Margaret and David Williams, thank you for your endless support and for patience during another year of all-consuming cookbook writing. Special thanks to Victoria's mom for her quick in-and-out hair-styling visits and for always being an inspiration. Much gratitude goes to her sisters and best friends, Katrina and Brianne Walsh, for support and for always being there. More gratitude to them and Lee Merwin for the many bar gifts and the feedback that got us started.

A shout-out to the rest of our families, whose excitement about our project kept us energized: the Jarvies, Millets, McCallums, Nixons and Williamses. Extra special recognition to Grandma McCallum for inspiring Scott's green thumb and to Lou Lou Williams for encouragement and talks about borage and lovage. Grandma and Papa Betty and Bill Jarvie, who would have loved this book. Grandma and Grandpa Nixon, for aggie blood. Marion Park, who supplied the gold chariot that enabled us to make so many of these long journeys.

We've leaned on so many friends along the way, and owe big thanks to our taste testers, who lent their palates and helped keep our livers less taxed—you know who you are (even if the memories are fuzzy). Special thanks to our dear friend and neighbour Michael for putting up with never-ending ice shaking at random hours but mostly for always being a life support. Maureen Halushak, for being a personal editor and a guide and writing teacher over the years. To her and her husband, Jeremy, for a computer loan, cocktail samplings and occasionally acting as our personal rum-runners. Our writer/editor friends, Brunch Club, who are always encouraging and inspiring. And a toast to George Kiddel and friends for way too many Manhattans and an introduction to Chartreuse.

Going back to the beginning, so many gracious and talented people helped make this book come to be. Huge thanks to Philina Chan and Steve Balaban for helping us pitch the proposal for our book and for helping to make the mini-book so stunning (and for Philina's work on canadiancocktail.com). Also to supremely talented photographer Juan Luna. Words cannot express our gratitude for his beautiful photography work and for all of his time and dedication. And tremendous thanks to Virginie Martocq who perfectly filled the frames with her supremely creative and dazzling prop styling. Also to her wonderful family for sharing their home for shoot days.

We are ever grateful to Penguin Random House Canada and Appetite's Robert McCullough and Lindsay Paterson for seeing the potential in our humble project and allowing us this exciting opportunity. A profound thank you to our editor, Kiara Kent, for all of her thoughtful and smart edits, patience and support. Supreme thanks to Scott Richardson for designing these beautiful pages, which far exceeded our high expectations. Thank you to Susan Burns for keeping the book on track. Susan Traxel, for lending an ear to this quirky little idea and putting us in touch with our publisher. And much thanks to our fantastic agent, Judy Linden, and Stonesong.

This project allowed us many excuses to travel and see Canada, and several people played a part in these wonderful trip experiences: Tara Sullivan, Avi Miller, the Craigs, Kat Tancock, Shelley McArthur, Sarah Lusk and Amy Watkins, Jennifer Danter, Louise Healy, and Jim Olver and the Banff Centre.

Special thanks to the staff and owners at The Yukon bar, for being so accommodating and allowing us to photograph our Loose Jaw cocktail in their beautiful bar. Huge gratitude to Kristen Voisey of BYOB Cocktail Emporium and her staff for loaning us so many cocktail supplies and gorgeous glassware.

Major thanks to all the distillers, bartenders and craftspeople who contributed to and are featured within these pages. Thank you for allowing us to include some of your own amazing recipes and for responding to our endless queries.

The 52%, 166
66 Gilead Distillery, 23, 118
1749 Negroni, 158

Aalborg Jubilaeums Akvavit, 90, 117
absinthe
    The Coupe de Cartier, 141
Acadian Driftwood, 142
aged rum, 9
Agg, Jen, 94, 113
Alberta Premium Dark Horse
    (Canadian whisky), 14, 70, 108
Alberta Springs, 127
The Alchemist, 119
allspice dram
    Hot Toddy, 17
amaro
    A Bit of Northern Hospitality, 70
    The Bush Pilot, 176
    The Polar Vortex, 121
    PTB, 103
amber rum
    The Nellie J. Banks, 148
amontillado sherry
    1749 Negroni, 158
    PTB, 103
Añejo Restaurant, 64
Angelica (Matos Winery & Distillery),
    135, 147
Angostura bitters. See also aromatic
    bitters
    about, 9
    1749 Negroni, 158
    Acadian Driftwood, 142
    Balsam Blend, 101
    Butchart Garden Swizzle, 61
    The Canadian, 14
    Cold Buttered Rum, 162
    The Double Double, 31
    Lord Stanley's Punch, 87
    Nan's Kitchen, 167
    The Nellie J. Banks, 148
    Ogopogo Sour, 49
    Pumpkin Colada, 156
    Smoky Lake Old-Fashioned, 58
    St. John's Sling, 164
    The Torontonian, 106
    Whoop-Up Bug Juice, 68
Aperol
    Arctic Martinez, 175
    Devil's Barrel, 83
    The Post Sunset, 151
    Watermelon and Campari–Infused
        Tequila, 50
Apple Butter, 162
apple cider
    Hot Buttered Rum, 160
apple juice

Apple Syrup, 121
    Bonita Applebaum, 76
    The Polar Vortex, 121
apples, uses for in cocktails, 200. See
    also apple cider; apple juice
Appleton Estate 12 Year Old Jamaica
    Rum, 158
apricot liqueur
    The Corroded Nail, 159
    The Oenophile, 46
    PTB, 103
aquavit
    Golden Boy, 90
    Prince Edward Bounty, 117
    Sea Island Iced Tea, 42
Arctic Martinez, 175
Arctic Rose Vermouth Reduction, 175
aromatic bitters. See also Angostura
    bitters; celery bitters; cherry bitters;
    grapefruit bitters; lavender bitters;
    mole bitters; orange bitters
    about, 9
    Acadian Driftwood, 142
    Bob & Doug's Strange Brew, 52
    Butchart Garden Swizzle, 61
    The Canadian, 14
    Caribou, 120
    The Gardiner, 108
    Gins & Needles, 77
    The Loose Jaw, 81
    North of 44, 111
    The Oenophile, 46
    Peary Punch, 110
    The Polar Vortex, 121
    Ronald Clayton, 107
    Sunken Port, 53
Artisan SakeMaker, 36
Atwater Market, 97
AuraGin (Yukon Shine Distillery), 23,
    175, 176
Aviation cocktail. See The Bush Pilot
Ayden Kitchen and Bar, 83

Bacardi 151 overproof rum, 148
Bain, David, 64
bakeapples. See cloudberries
    (bakeapples); cloudberry liqueur
Balsam Blend, 101
Balsam Fir Syrup, 183
Bar Buca, 95
Bärenjäger Honey Liqueur, 90
Bar Isabel, 94
barley
    The Pearl Punch, 73
Barley Days Brewery, 95
Bar Raval, 94, 106
bee balm, uses for in cocktails, 198
Beefeater London dry gin, 9, 140
Beehan, Shane, 135, 155
bee pollen

Chinook Sangria, 71
beer. See also ginger beer; radler;
    wheat beer
    A Bit of Northern Hospitality, 70
    Bob & Doug's Strange Brew, 52
    Pilsner Infusion, 70
    Rich Stout Syrup, 52
    Saison Royale, 122
bell peppers. See peppers
Bellwoods Brewery, 95
Benedictine
    St. John's Sling, 164
berries, uses for in cocktails. See
    individual types
The Bicycle Thief, 135
Big Spruce Brewing, 136
Bin Brewing, 65
birch syrup. See also maple syrup
    The Bush Pilot, 176
A Bit of Northern Hospitality, 70
Bittered Sling bitters, 9, 14, 46, 49, 52,
    53, 54, 56, 61, 110, 111, 142, 195
bitters. See Angostura bitters; aromatic
    bitters
Bitter Truth bitters, 17, 130
Black Beaux-Arts Fizz, 128
blackberries
    Blackberry Grenadine, 189
    Whisky-Soaked Wild Fruit, 101
Blackbird Public House, 46
black currant liqueur. See Crème de
    Cassis
Black Grouse blended Scotch, 103
Black Sesame Syrup, 102
Black Tea Syrup, 70
Black Walnut Orgeat, 192
blueberries. See also blueberry liqueur
    The 52%, 166
    Canadian Fruit Shrub, 28
    The Loyalist, 140
    Rich Blueberry Syrup, 183
    Whisky-Soaked Wild Fruit, 101
    Wild Blueberry Shrub, 166
blueberry liqueur
    Lavender-Blueberry Sparkler, 152
Blue Curacao. See also Dry Curacao
    The Boreal Cotton-Candy Cocktail,
        125
Blue Mountain Vineyards and Cellars,
    64
Bluenose Black Rum (Ironworks
    Distillery), 152, 156
Bob & Doug's Strange Brew, 52
Boker's aromatic bitters, 9
Bombay Peggy's, 170
Bonita Applebaum, 76
borage
    about, 99, 198
    Pimm's Spin, 99
The Boreal Cotton-Candy Cocktail, 125

Boudreau, Josh, 37
Boulevard Kitchen & Oyster Bar, 42
bourbon
    about, 10
    Bonita Applebaum, 76
    Hot Toddy, 17
    Jack with One Eye, 41
    Yukon Gold Rush, 173
Bourbon Room, 76
brandy. See also eau de vie
    Campfire Flip, 59
    Canadian Cocktail Cherries, 188
The Bright Red, 145
Brown Butter–Infused Unaged Whisky,
    185
Buffalo Trace Bourbon, 17
Bullshot. See The Stampeder
The Bush Pilot, 176
Bushwakker Brewpub, 65–66
Butchart Garden Swizzle, 61
BYOB Cocktail Emporium, 167

Cabane à Sucre Au Pied de Cochon, 96
Caesars
    East–Meets–West Coast, 19
    The Great White, 18
    Prairie, 86
    The Stampeder, 78
Café Medina, 195
calvados
    Caribou, 120
    Devil's Barrel, 83
    Saison Royale, 122
camelina oil
    Golden Boy, 90
Campari
    1749 Negroni, 158
    The Loyalist, 140
    Spadina Splash, 104
    Watermelon and Campari–Infused
        Tequila, 50
    Wild Rose Negroni, 150
Campfire Flip, 59
The Canadian, 14
Canadian Club (Canadian whisky), 121,
    144, 185
Canadian Cocktail Cherries, 188
Canadian Fruit Shrub, 28
The Canadian R&R, 114
Canadian Rye Dirty Martini, 118
Canadian whisky
    about, 10
    Balsam Blend, 101
    A Bit of Northern Hospitality, 70
    Black Walnut Orgeat, 192
    Campfire Flip, 59
    The Canadian, 14
    Canadian Cocktail Cherries, 188
    Canadian Winter's Punch, 44
    Devil's Barrel, 83

The Double Double, 31
Jack with One Eye, 41
The Loose Jaw, 81
Lord Stanley's Punch, 87
Magnetic Hill Winery, 144
Man About Chinatown, 102
The Pearl Punch, 73
Pine-Infused Canadian Whisky, 185
The Polar Vortex, 121
Ronald Clayton, 107
Saskatoon Julep, 43
Saucier's Seigniory Special, 127
Smoky Lake Old-Fashioned, 58
The Torontonian, 106
Vanilla-Infused Lot No. 40
    Canadian Whisky, 107
Whisky-Soaked Wild Fruit, 101
The Yukon Sourtoe Shot, 178
Canadian Winter's Punch, 44
Cann, Dylan, 64
Cape Breton Farmers' Market, 136
Caramelized Parsnip, 119
Caribou, 120
Carpano Antica Formula (vermouth), 9,
    108
carrot juice
    What's Up, Doc? 54
Cassis Monna & Filles, 25, 97
Catalano Restaurant & Cicchetti Bar, 37
Caudle, Nate, 43
celery. See also celery bitters
    Celery Rickey, 113
    Celery-Verjus Shrub, 113
    Tomato-Clam Juice, 193
celery bitters
    The Emperor, 56
    La Pomme du Diable, 130
    The Oenophile, 46
    What's Up, Doc? 54
Chambord
    The Bright Red, 145
Charcut restaurant, 83
Chardonnay-Maple Reduction, 47
Charlottetown Farmers' Market, 135
Chartreuse
    about, 130
    Celery Rickey, 113
    The Gardiner, 108
    La Pomme du Diable, 130
Château Montebello, 127
Chell, Walter, 18
cherries. See also cherry bitters; cherry
    liqueur; maraschino liqueur
    as garnish, 6, 41
    Canadian Cocktail Cherries, 188
    Canadian Fruit Shrub, 28
cherry bitters
    Ogopogo Sour, 49
cherry liqueur. See also maraschino
    liqueur

Jack with One Eye, 41
    Ogopogo Sour, 49
Chicoutai cloudberry liqueur, 164
Chili Syrup, 76
Chilled Earl Grey Tea, 44
Chilled Labrador Tea, 163
Chinook Arch Meadery, 71
Chinook Sangria, 71
Cho, Christopher, 83
Chovancek, Jonathan, 56, 195
cider. See apple cider
Cidrerie et Vergers Pedneault, 25, 84,
    97
cinchona bark
    Tonic, 186
Cinnamon Syrup, 182
Cinzano (vermouth), 56, 108
citrus. See individual types
clam juice
    Tomato-Clam Juice, 193
Classic Negroni, 150
Clive's Classic Lounge, 37
cloudberries (bakeapples). See also
    cloudberry liqueur
    about, 164
    Bakeapple Compound Butter, 160
cloudberry liqueur
    The Corroded Nail, 159
    St. John's Sling, 164
club soda, 114
    The Boreal Cotton-Candy Cocktail,
        125
    The Bright Red, 145
    Butchart Garden Swizzle, 61
    The Canadian R&R, 114
    Celery Rickey, 113
    Chinook Sangria, 71
    Cold Buttered Rum, 162
    The Flatlander's Fizz, 82
    Gin & Tonic, 22
    Lord Stanley's Punch, 87
    The Nellie J. Banks, 148
    The Spell of the Yukon, 177
    St. John's Sling, 164
    Sweet Fern G&T, 126
Cocktail Cherries, Canadian, 188
Coconut Pumpkin Butter, 156
coffee
    Jack with One Eye, 41
Cointreau
    about, 9
    Jack with One Eye, 41
    Labrador Iced Tea, 163
    St. John's Sling, 164
cola
    Whoop-Up Bug Juice, 68
Cold Buttered Rum, 162
Cold Tea (bar), 94
Concord grapes
    Canadian Fruit Shrub, 28

Cordial, Raspberry, 190
Cormier, Jenner, 151
Corriveau, Martin, 36
The Corroded Nail, 159
Coster's Prescription Coffee and A
    Smoke Bitters, 121
County Cider Company, 95
The Coupe de Cartier, 141
cranberry juice
    Sea Island Iced Tea, 42
cream liqueur
    The Double Double, 31
Crème de Cassis
    about, 25
    Canadian producers of, 25
    Kir, 24
    Kir Royale, 24
Crème de Petites Poire (Cidrerie et
    Vergers Pedneault), 25, 84
crème de violette
    Butchart Garden Swizzle, 61
Crowfoot Wine & Spirits, 64
Crown Royal, 66, 87
Cruz, Alexander, 163
cucumbers
    uses for in cocktails, 200
    The Emperor, 56
    Pimm's Spin, 99
Curacao. See Blue Curacao; Dry
    Curacao

DaiLo, 95
Dandelion and Burdock Bitters, Dr.
    Adam Elmegirab's, 120
dark rum
    about, 68
    Canadian Winter's Punch, 44
    Hot Buttered Rum, 160
    Pumpkin Colada, 156
    Saucier's Seigniory Special, 127
    Tobacco Syrup, 107
    Whoop-Up Bug Juice, 68
dates
    Ginseng & Red Date Syrup, 104
Designer Cocktail Company, 58
dessert wine
    Magnetic Hill Winery, 144
Devil's Barrel, 83
The Diamond, 36
Diamond Tooth Gerties Gambling
    Hall, 170–71
Dieu du Ciel, 97
Dillon's Small Batch Distillers, 23, 95,
    108, 111
Distillerie Fils du Roy, 23, 25, 134, 139,
    141, 152
Dolin de Chambéry (vermouth), 9, 77
Domaine de la Vallée du Bras, 97
Domaine Pinnacle Microdistillerie, 23,
    96, 130

Dominion Square Tavern, 96–97
Don Julio Blanco (tequila), 151
d'Origina Être boréal, 96
The Double Double, 31
Downtown Hotel, 171
Dr. Adam Elmegirab's Dandelion and
    Burdock Bitters, 120
Drake Hotel, 95
The Drawing Room, 135
Dry Curacao. See also Blue Curacao
    about, 9
    Chinook Sangria, 71
    Sparkling Watermelon Sipper, 147
dry vermouth. See vermouth
Dulse-Salt Rimmer, 19

Earl Grey tea
    Canadian Winter's Punch, 44
    Earl Grey–Infused Rum, 166
    Pilsner Infusion, 70
East–Meets–West Coast Caesar, 19
Eau Claire Distillery, 23, 64, 71, 78
eau de vie. See also brandy
    Canadian Cocktail Cherries, 188
    The Oenophile, 46
    Pear-Infused Vermouth, 56
Edna, 135
eggs
    The 52%, 166
    Black Beaux-Arts Fizz, 128
    The Boreal Cotton-Candy Cocktail,
    125
    Campfire Flip, 59
    Man About Chinatown, 102
    North of 44, 111
    Ogopogo Sour, 49
    Saison Royale, 122
    Saucier's Seigniory Special, 127
Eileanan Brèagha Vineyards, 136
El Camino 2.0, 50
elderflower liqueur
    Prince Edward Bounty, 117
    The Torontonian, 106
Elves, Chuck, 64, 77
The Emerald, 97
The Emperor, 56
evaporated milk
    Nan's Kitchen, 167

Fernet Branca
    Gins & Needles, 77
    The Torontonian, 106
Fiddlehead Martini, 139
Fiddleheads, Lemony Pickled, 139
Field Guide, 135
Field Stone, 25
Fig Syrup, 108
Fireweed Community Market, 177
fireweed honey, about, 173
flaming citrus oils, 6

The Flatlander's Fizz, 82
Flaxseed Rimmer, Toasted, 86
Flintabbatey Flonatin's Sunless City
    Sipper, 89
flowers, uses for in cocktails, 200. See
    also herbs, uses for in cocktails
Fogo Island Inn, 136, 166
foraged garnishes and ingredients,
    safety of, 6
Forbidden Fruit Winery, 38
Forty Creek Distillery, 31, 43, 83
French vermouth. See vermouth
Fruit, Whisky-Soaked Wild, 101
fruit liqueurs, 25. See also individual
    types
fruits and vegetables for cocktails, 200.
    See also individual types
Fruit Shrub, Canadian, 28

The Gardiner, 108
genever. See gin
Geraldine, 94, 108
geraniums, uses for in cocktails, 200
Gerard Lounge, 42
Gibson's Finest 12 Year Old Canadian
    Whisky, 58
Giffard Abricot de Roussillon, 46
gin
    about, 9
    Canadian producers of, 23
    and oysters, 195
    The Alchemist, 119
    Arctic Martinez, 175
    Black Beaux-Arts Fizz, 128
    The Bush Pilot, 176
    Celery Rickey, 113
    The Coupe de Cartier, 141
    The Emperor, 56
    Fiddlehead Martini, 139
    The Flatlander's Fizz, 82
    Gin & Tonic, 22
    Gins & Needles, 77
    Labrador Iced Tea, 163
    Lavender-Blueberry Sparkler, 152
    Lavender-Infused Gin, 184
    The Loyalist, 140
    North of 44, 111
    The Pearl Punch, 73
    Peary Punch, 110
    Rocket Richardonnay, 47
    Sour Slush, 28
    Spadina Splash, 104
    Spiced Peach Spritz, 74
    Sunken Port, 53
    Sweet Fern G&T, 126
    Wild Rose Negroni, 150
    Winter Garden, 155
ginger. See also ginger ale; ginger beer
uses for in cocktails, 198
    Ginger-Infused Honey Syrup, 42

Ginger Syrup, 182
Peary Punch, 110
ginger ale
    The Loose Jaw, 81
    Pimm's Spin, 99
ginger beer
    The 52%, 166
    Flintabbatey Flonatin's Sunless City
      Sipper, 89
    Ginger Beer Syrup, 166
    La Pomme du Diable, 130
    Spiced Peach Spritz, 74
Gins & Needles, 77
Ginseng & Red Date Syrup, 104
Gin Thuya (Distillerie Fils du Roy), 23,
    139, 141
Glen Breton Rare 10 Year (Scotch), 159
Glenora Distillery, 136, 159
Golden Boy, 90
Goodfellow, Robin, 94, 106
Goyet, Dominic, 122
Grande Bagosse (Distillerie Fils du
    Roy), 139
Grand Marnier
    about, 9
    Nan's Kitchen, 167
The Grange of Prince Edward Vineyard
    and Estate Winery, 95
Granville Island, 36
grapefruit and grapefruit juice. See also
    grapefruit bitters; grapefruit radler
    Devil's Barrel, 83
    North of 44, 111
    Saucier's Seigniory Special, 127
    Spadina Splash, 104
    Sweet Fern Tonic Syrup, 126
    Tonic, 186
grapefruit bitters
    Bob & Doug's Strange Brew, 52
    Devil's Barrel, 83
grapefruit radler
    El Camino 2.0, 50
grapes. See Concord grapes
Gray, Ryan, 121
Gray Monk Estate Winery, 38, 53
Great Canadian Cheese Festival, 95
Great Western Brewing, 65
The Great White Caesar, 18
green Chartreuse. See Chartreuse
green tea
    Sea Island Iced Tea, 42
Greig, David, 113
grenadine
    Black Beaux-Arts Fizz, 128
Grenadine, Blackberry, 189
Grenadine, Traditional-Style, 189

Half Pints Brewing, 65, 84
Halifax Seaport Farmers' Market, 135
Happy Knight, 25

Harbord Room, 95, 107
Haskap Liqueur (LB Distillers), 25
Havana Club (rum), 68, 107, 114
Hawksworth Restaurant, 14
Head, Nathan, 64, 70
Hendrick's Gin, 74
herbs, uses for in cocktails, 6, 8, 198.
    See also flowers, uses for in
    cocktails; and individual types
Holl-Allen, Robert, 59
Holy Spirits Gin (Silver Sperling
    Distillery), 23
honey. See also honey liqueur; mead
    as headache remedy, 71
    Black Sesame Syrup, 102
    Ginger-Infused Honey Syrup,
      42
    Honey Syrup, 183
    Hot Buttered Rum, 160
honey liqueur
    Golden Boy, 90
honey wine. See mead
Hoof Cocktail Bar, 94, 113
Hot Buttered Rum, 160
Hotel Arts, 64
Hotel Herman, 96, 122
Hot Toddy, 17
House Spruce Liqueur, 77

Ice Cider (Domaine Pinnacle), 130
Iced Tea, Labrador, 163
Iced Tea, Sea Island, 42
Icewine Festival (Ontario), 95
infusions
    about, 184
    fruits, vegetables, and flowers used
      in, 200
    Brown Butter–Infused Unaged
      Whisky, 185
    Lavender-Infused Gin, 184
    Pilsner Infusion, 70
    Pine-Infused Canadian Whisky, 185
    Seamist Tea–Infused Vodka, 184
Irish whiskey
    about, 10
    The Yukon Sourtoe Shot, 178
Ironworks Distillery, 25, 84, 136, 156
Italian vermouth. See vermouth

Jack with One Eye, 41
jalapeños. See also peppers
    Bob & Doug's Strange Brew, 52
Jamaica Rum (Appleton Estate), 158
Jameson Irish Whiskey, 178
Jean Talon Market, 97
Jensen, Micah, 38, 47
Joe Beef, 96, 121
Johnny Ziegler Brandy (Winegarden
    Estate), 134
Jones, Jay, 46

J.R.'s Dry Organic Canadian Gin
    (Toronto Distillery Co.), 23

Kahlúa
    The Double Double, 31
Kaufman, Robin, 102
Keefer Bar, 58
Kensington Market, 94
Kergommeaux, Davin de, 118
King Arthur's Dry Mead (Chinook Arch
    Meadery), 71
Kir, 24
Kir Royale, 24
kirsch
    Canadian Cocktail Cherries, 188
    Ogopogo Sour, 49
Koshihikari Rice, Toasted, & Sesame
    Syrup, 56
Kraken Black Spiced Rum, 127, 156

L'Abattoir, 36–37
Labrador Iced Tea, 163
La Courailleuse (Distillerie Fils du Roy),
    141
La Ferme Basque, 97
La Frenz Winery, 38
lager. See beer
Lamb's Palm Breeze (spiced rum), 162,
    167
La Pentola, 36
Laphroaig Quarter Cask Scotch, 142
La Pomme du Diable, 130
Lapponia cloudberry liqueur, 164
LaStella Fortissimo, 46
Last Mountain Distillery, 66
lavender. See also lavender bitters
    Lavender-Blueberry Sparkler, 152
    Lavender-Infused Gin, 184
    Peach & Lavender Shrub, 74
lavender bitters
    Spiced Peach Spritz, 74
Layton, Shaun, 37, 50
LB Distillers, 25, 82, 84
Leacock, Stephen, 17
Left Coast Hemp Vodka (Victoria Spirits),
    61, 184
Le Lab Comptoir à Cocktails, 96, 119
Le Marché des Saveurs du Québec, 97
lemongrass
    Tonic, 186
lemons and lemon juice
    A Bit of Northern Hospitality, 70
    The Bright Red, 145
    The Bush Pilot, 176
    Butchart Garden Swizzle, 61
    The Canadian, 14
    Canadian Cocktail Cherries, 188
    Canadian Winter's Punch, 44
    Chinook Sangria, 71
    Cold Buttered Rum, 162

The Coupe de Cartier, 141
Devil's Barrel, 83
East–Meets–West Coast Caesar, 19
The Flatlander's Fizz, 82
Flintabbatey Flonatin's Sunless City
    Sipper, 89
Golden Boy, 90
The Great White Caesar, 18
Hot Toddy, 17
ice ring, 87
Labrador Iced Tea, 163
Lavender-Blueberry Sparkler, 152
Lemony Pickled Fiddleheads, 139
Lord Stanley's Punch, 84
Magnetic Hill Sour, 144
Man About Chinatown, 102
The Nellie J. Banks, 148
Ogopogo Sour, 49
Peach & Lavender Shrub, 74
The Pearl Punch, 73
The Polar Vortex, 121
Prairie Caesar, 86
Rocket Richardonnay, 47
Saison Royale, 122
Saskatoon Berry & Wheat Beer
    Cocktail, 84
Saucier's Seigniory Special, 127
Sea Island Iced Tea, 42
Smoky Lake Old-Fashioned, 58
Sparkling Watermelon Sipper, 147
Spiced Peach Spritz, 74
The Stampeder, 78
St. John's Sling, 164
Tomato-Clam Juice, 193
Tonic, 186
Whoop-Up Bug Juice, 68
Winter Garden, 155
Yukon Gold Rush, 173
lemon verbena, uses for in cocktails,
    198
Les Distillateurs Subversifs
    Microdistillerie, 23, 96, 119
Les Douceurs du Marché, 97
Le Souverain Bleu (Distillerie Fils du
    Roy), 25
Lillet
    The Bright Red, 145
    The Loyalist, 140
limes and lime juice
    The Alchemist, 119
    Black Beaux-Arts Fizz, 128
    Bob & Doug's Strange Brew, 52
    Bonita Applebaum, 76
    The Boreal Cotton-Candy Cocktail,
        125
    The Canadian R&R, 114
    Celery Rickey, 113
    East–Meets–West Coast Caesar, 19
    El Camino 2.0, 50
    Gin & Tonic, 22

The Great White Caesar, 18
La Pomme du Diable, 130
Magnetic Hill Sour, 144
The Nellie J. Banks, 148
Pimm's Spin, 99
The Post Sunset, 151
The Spell of the Yukon, 177
Spiced Cinnamon Syrup, 182
Sweet Fern G&T, 126
Sweet Fern Tonic Syrup, 126
Tonic, 186
Limoncello
    The Post Sunset, 151
liqueurs, storage of homemade, 185.
    See also individual types
Little Jumbo, 43
London dry gin. See gin
Long Table Distillery, 23
The Loose Jaw, 81
LoPan, 95
Lord Stanley's Punch, 87
L'Orléane Cassis de L'Île d'Orléans, 25
Lot No. 40 Canadian Whisky, 102, 106,
    107
lovage
    about, 198
    Lovage-Salt Rimmer, 18
    Tomato-Clam Juice, 193
The Loyalist, 140
Loyalist Gin (66 Gilead Distillery), 23
Lucky Bastards Distillers, 66
Luksic, Jacob, 136, 166
Luxardo Apricot Liqueur, 103

Magnetic Hill Sour, 144
Magnetic Hill Winery, 144
Magnolia Hotel, 37
Mah, Christina, 64, 74
Maison Publique, 96
Man About Chinatown, 102
Manhattan. See The Loose Jaw
Maple Leaf Spirits, 38, 49
maple liqueur
    Acadian Driftwood, 142
    Saucier's Seigniory Special, 127
maple syrup. See also birch syrup;
    maple liqueur
    The Alchemist, 119
    Caramelized Parsnip, 119
    Caribou, 120
    Chardonnay-Maple Reduction, 47
    Lord Stanley's Punch, 87
    Maple Marshmallow Syrup, 59
    Maple-Port Reduction, 120
    Peary Punch, 110
    Saucier's Seigniory Special, 127
maraschino liqueur. See also cherry
    liqueur
    The Bush Pilot, 176
    Canadian Cocktail Cherries, 188

Marché du Vieux-Port, 97
Martinez, Arctic, 175
Martini, Canadian Rye Dirty, 118
Martini, Fiddlehead, 139
Matos Winery & Distillery, 135, 147
McDonald, Katie, 37, 38, 53
mead
    about, 71
    blackberry mead (Bushwakker
        Brewpub), 65
    Chinook Sangria, 71
Meyer lemons. See lemons and lemon
    juice
mezcal. See also tequila
    Bob & Doug's Strange Brew, 52
Michel Jodoin Calijo, 120
Microbrasserie Le Trou du Diable, 122
milk. See evaporated milk
Milk Tiger Lounge, 64, 70
Mill St. Brewery, 84, 95
mint
    The Alchemist, 119
    Butchart Garden Swizzle, 61
    Saskatoon Julep, 43
    Seamist Tea–Infused Vodka, 184
Mitton, Dave, 95, 107, 111
Model Milk, 64, 76
mole bitters
    Jack with One Eye, 41
Mondia Alliance, 25
Mooney, Michael, 94, 108
morel mushrooms
    Pickled Morel Mushrooms, 178
    The Yukon Sourtoe Shot, 178
Moscow Mule. See Flintabbatey
    Flonatin's Sunless City Sipper
Mote, Lauren, 36, 56
Mount Gay Eclipse Barbados Rum, 54
mushrooms. See morel mushrooms
mustard, Canadian, 117
Myriad View Artisan Distillery, 135, 148

Nan's Kitchen, 167
nasturtiums, uses for in cocktails, 200
navy rum, 9
Negroni, 1749, 158
Negroni, Classic, 150
Negroni, Wild Rose, 150
The Nellie J. Banks, 148
Newfoundland Screech Rum, 160, 164
Niagara Riesling, 110
Noble, 135, 151
Nora Gray, 121
Norman Hardie Winery and Vineyard,
    95
North of 44, 111
Northwood, 95
Notturno, 59

Odd Society Spirits, 25

Odyssey III (Gray Monk Estate Winery), 38, 53
The Oenophile, 46
Ogden, Simon, 37, 54
Ogopogo Sour, 49
Okanagan Spirits, 23, 25, 38, 42, 46, 47, 56, 82
Old-Fashioned. *See* Smoky Lake Old-Fashioned; The Canadian
Old Fort Brewery, 52
Old Italian Prune Brandy Eau de Vie (Okanagan Spirits), 46
Old Style Pilsner, 70
Old Tom gin. *See* gin
olive oil
    Golden Boy, 90
Omerto (Domaine de la Vallée du Bras), 97
Ontario Spring Water Sake Company, 95, 104
Opus Hotel, 36
orange bitters, 9
    The Corroded Nail, 159
    Peary Punch, 110
    PTB, 103
    The Spell of the Yukon, 177
    St. John's Sling, 164
orange blossom water
    Black Walnut Orgeat, 192
orange liqueur, 9. *See also* Cointreau; Dry Curacao; Grand Marnier; Triple Sec
oranges and orange juice. *See also* orange bitters; orange blossom water; orange liqueur
    1749 Negroni, 158
    Canadian Cocktail Cherries, 188
    Canadian Winter's Punch, 44
    Caribou, 120
    The Corroded Nail, 159
    ice ring, 87
    Lord Stanley's Punch, 87
    The Loyalist, 140
    Man About Chinatown, 102
    Nan's Kitchen, 167
    The Pearl Punch, 73
    The Post Sunset, 151
    Pumpkin Colada, 156
    St. John's Sling, 164
    The Torontonian, 106
    Wild Rose Negroni, 150
orgeat
    Black Beaux-Arts Fizz, 128
    Black Walnut Orgeat, 192
    Ogopogo Sour, 49
Osake Fraser Valley Junmai Nigori Sake, 56
overproof rum, 9
Oyama Sausage Co., 36

Panaccio, Gabrielle, 119
Parlour Gin (Eau Claire Distillery), 23
Parniak, Sarah, 94, 103
Parsnip, Caramelized, 119
partridgeberry jelly
    Nan's Kitchen, 167
Paulson, Thor, 36
peaches
    Canadian Fruit Shrub, 28
    Peach & Lavender Shrub, 74
Pear Eau de Vie (Ironworks Distillery), 152
Pear-Infused Vermouth, 56
The Pearl Punch, 73
Peary Punch, 110
Peoples Eatery, 94
peppers. *See also* jalapeños
    uses for in cocktails, 200
    Whoop-Up Bug Juice, 68
Perfect Manhattan. *See* The Loose Jaw
Pernod Absinthe, 141
Perrier
    The Alchemist, 119
Peychaud's Bitters, 9
Phillips Brewing Elsinore Lager, 52
Phipps, Stephen, 76
Picaroons Brewing Company, 134
Pickled Morel Mushrooms, 178
Piger Henricus Gin (Les Distillateurs Subversifs Microdistillerie), 23, 96, 119
Pilsner Infusion, 70
pimento dram (Bitter Truth), 17
Pimm's Spin, 99
Piña Colada. *See* Pumpkin Colada
pineapple and pineapple juice
    Canadian Winter's Punch, 44
    Nan's Kitchen, 167
    Pumpkin Colada, 156
    St. John's Sling, 164
Pine-Infused Canadian Whisky, 185
pisco
    The Bright Red, 145
    Rhubarb-Infused Pisco, 177
    The Spell of the Yukon, 177
plum & rootbeer bitters
    Sunken Port, 53
Poire Williams Eau de Vie (Okanagan Spirits), 56
The Polar Vortex, 121
pomegranates
    Traditional-Style Grenadine, 189
port
    Caribou, 120
    Maple-Port Reduction, 120
    Sunken Port, 53
Porter, Brant, 37
The Post Sunset, 151
Prairie Caesar, 86
Prairie Sun Brewery, 65, 84

premium aged rum, 9
Prince Edward Bounty, 117
Pritchard, John, 135, 150
Proof (brand), 114, 178
Propeller Brewing Company, 135
Prosecco. *See also* sparkling wine
    The Post Sunset, 151
prune brandy
    The Oenophile, 46
PTB, 103
pumpkins
    Coconut Pumpkin Butter, 156
    Pumpkin Colada, 156
punches
    ice rings for, 87
    Canadian Winter's, 44
    Lord Stanley's, 87
    The Pearl, 73
    Peary, 110
Pur Vodka, 125

radler
    El Camino 2.0, 50
raspberries. *See also* raspberry liqueur
    Raspberry Cordial, 190
    Whisky-Soaked Wild Fruit, 101
Raspberry Dessert Wine (Magnetic Hill Winery), 144
raspberry liqueur
    The Bright Red, 145
Ratinaud French Cuisine, 135
RauDZ Regional Table, 38, 47
Raw Bar by Duncan Ly, 64, 74
Red Rooster, 47
red wine. *See also* port
    The Bright Red, 145
    Caribou, 120
    The Oenophile, 46
rhubarb
    as garnish, 114
    Canadian Fruit Shrub, 28
    Rhubarb-Infused Pisco, 177
    Rhubarb-Peppercorn Syrup, 183
    The Spell of the Yukon, 177
Rhubarb Esprit (Ironworks Distillery), 25, 152
rhum agricole, 9
Rich Blueberry Syrup, 183
Rich Stout Syrup, 52
Rich Syrup, 183
Riesling Syrup, 111
Riga Black Balsam liqueur
    Flintabbatey Flonatin's Sunless City Sipper, 89
rimmers
    bee pollen rimmer, 71
    Dulse-Salt Rimmer, 19
    Lovage-Salt Rimmer, 18
    Toasted Flaxseed Rimmer, 86
Road 13 Vineyards, 38

Rocket Richardonnay, 47
Rodney's Oyster House, 195
Rodrigues Winery, 25, 159, 164
Ronald Clayton, 107
rose liqueur
    Wild Rose Negroni, 150
rosemary
    The Gardiner, 108
roses. *See also* rose liqueur; rosewater
    uses for in cocktails, 200
    Arctic Rose Vermouth Reduction,
        175
rosewater
    Winter Garden, 155
Rosewood Hotel Georgia, 14
Rossignol, John, 135
Rossignol Estate Winery, 25, 135, 150
Roy, Sébastien, 134
rum. *See also* allspice dram; amber
    rum; dark rum; Newfoundland
    Screech Rum; spiced rum; white
    rum
    about, 9
    1749 Negroni, 158
    Sour Slush, 28
    Turmeric-Infused Rum, 54
    What's Up, Doc? 54
Rusty Nail. *See* The Corroded Nail
rye whisky. *See* Canadian whisky

sage
    Bonita Applebaum, 76
    La Pomme du Diable, 130
Saison du Tracteur beer
    (Microbrasserie Le Trou du Diable),
        122
Saison Royale, 122
sake
    The Emperor, 56
    Spadina Splash, 104
Saline, 113
Salted Brick, 38
sangrias
    Chinook, 71
    The Oenophile, 46
Saskatoon berry liqueur
    Canadian producers of, 25
    Saskatoon Berry & Wheat Beer
        Cocktail, 84
    Saskatoon Julep, 43
Saskatoon Farmers' Market, 66
Saucier, Ted, 14, 127
Saucier's Seigniory Special, 127
Sax, Aja, 111
Scheffler's Delicatessen, 94
Scotch
    about, 10
    Acadian Driftwood, 142
    The Corroded Nail, 159
    Ogopogo Sour, 49

PTB, 103
    Winter Garden, 155
Scrappy's Cardamom Bitters, 77
sea buckthorn berries. *See also* sea
    buckthorn liqueur
    about, 82
    The Flatlander's Fizz, 82
sea buckthorn liqueur
    Canadian producers of, 25
    The Flatlander's Fizz, 82
    Sea Island Iced Tea, 42
Sea Island Iced Tea, 42
Seamist tea (Silk Road Tea)
    about, 61
    Seamist Tea–Infused Vodka, 184
The Seigniory Club, 127
Service, Robert, 177
sesame seeds
    Black Sesame Syrup, 102
    Sesame & Toasted Koshihikari Rice
        Syrup, 56
sherry. *See* amontillado sherry
Shiroki, Masa, 56
shochu
    The Pearl Punch, 73
shrubs
    Canadian Fruit, 28
    Celery-Verjus, 113
    Peach & Lavender, 74
    Wild Blueberry, 166
Siegel, T.J., 173
Silk Road Tea, 61, 184
Silver Sperling Distillery, 23
Simple Syrup, 182
Singapore Sling. *See* St. John's Sling
single malt whisky. *See* Scotch
Sismondo, Christine, 110
Slow Pub, 23, 65
Smith & Cross, 148
Smoked Spruce Syrup, 58
Smoky Lake Old-Fashioned, 58
Société-Orignal, 96, 163
Sortilège Canadian Whisky and Maple
    Syrup Liqueur, 127, 142
Sourdough Saloon, 171, 178
Sour Slush, 28
Sourtoe Cocktail, 171, 178. *See also* The
    Yukon Sourtoe Shot
Spadina Splash, 104
Sparkling Watermelon Sipper, 147
sparkling wine. *See also* Prosecco
    Kir Royale, 24
    Lavender-Blueberry Sparkler, 152
    Lord Stanley's Punch, 87
    Sparkling Watermelon Sipper, 147
The Spell of the Yukon, 177
Sperling Distillery, 66
Spiced Cinnamon Syrup, 182
Spiced Peach Spritz, 74
spiced rum

Cold Buttered Rum, 162
    Nan's Kitchen, 167
    Pumpkin Colada, 156
    Saucier's Seigniory Special, 127
spiced whisky, 10
Spirit Bear, 47, 77
Splash Parallel 49 Tricycle Grapefruit
    Radler, 50
Spruce Liqueur, House, 77
Spruce Syrup, Smoked, 58
The Stampeder, 78
Steeves, Chad, 144
St. Elizabeth allspice dram, 17
St-Germain Elderflower Liqueur, 106,
    117
Still Waters Distillery, 86, 96
St. John's Sling, 164
St. Lawrence Market, 94
Stout Syrup, Rich, 52
Strait Gin (Myriad View Artisan Distillery),
    23, 148
strawberries
    Canadian Fruit Shrub, 28
    Pimm's Spin, 99
    Whisky-Soaked Wild Fruit, 101
Strega liqueur, 90
Sunken Port, 53
Sutton Place Hotel, 42
Sweet Fern G&T, 126
Sweet Fern Tonic Syrup, 126
sweet vermouth. *See* vermouth
syrups
    Apple, 121
    Balsam Fir, 183
    Black Sesame, 102
    Black Tea, 70
    Chili, 76
    Cinnamon, 182
    Fig, 108
    Ginger, 182
    Ginger Beer, 166
    Ginger-Infused Honey, 42
    Ginseng & Red Date, 104
    Honey, 183
    Maple Marshmallow, 59
    Rhubarb-Peppercorn, 183
    Rich, 183
    Rich Blueberry, 183
    Rich Stout, 52
    Riesling, 111
    Simple, 182
    Smoked Spruce, 58
    Spiced Cinnamon, 182
    Sweet Fern Tonic, 126
    Toasted Koshihikari Rice & Sesame,
        56
    Tobacco, 107
    Tonic, 186

Tatarin, Danielle, 58

Tawse Winery, 95
Taylor, Justin, 42
tea
    A Bit of Northern Hospitality, 70
    Black Tea Syrup, 70
    Canadian Winter's Punch, 44
    Chilled Earl Grey Tea, 44
    Chilled Labrador Tea, 163
    Earl Grey–Infused Rum, 166
    Labrador Iced Tea, 163
    The Pearl Punch, 73
    Pilsner Infusion, 70
    Sea Island Iced Tea, 42
    Seamist Tea–Infused Vodka, 184
tequila
    El Camino 2.0, 50
    Labrador Iced Tea, 163
    La Pomme du Diable, 130
    The Post Sunset, 151
    Watermelon and Campari–Infused
        Tequila, 50
Terre Rouge, 135, 150
Thomas, Jerry, 44
THR and Co., 107
Three Boars Eatery, 64, 77
Three Farmers Camelina Oil, 90
Three Point Vodka (Eau Claire
    Distillery), 64, 71, 78
Tide and Boar, 134, 144
Tip of the Spear Spruce IPA (Big
    Spruce Brewing), 136
Toasted Flaxseed Rimmer, 86
Toasted Koshihikari Rice & Sesame
    Syrup, 56
Tobacco Syrup, 107
Tomato-Clam Juice, 193
    East–Meets–West Coast Caesar, 19
    The Great White Caesar, 18
    Prairie Caesar, 86
    The Stampeder, 78
tomatoes
    Tomato-Clam Juice, 193
tonic
    Gin & Tonic, 22
    homemade, 186
Tonic Syrup, Sweet Fern, 126
Toronto Distillery Co., 23
The Torontonian, 106
Toronto Temperance Society, 102
Traditional-Style Grenadine, 189
Triple Sec
    about, 9
    Jack with One Eye, 41
Turmeric-Infused Rum, 54

unaged whisky
    about, 10
    Brown Butter–Infused Unaged
        Whisky, 185
    Prairie Caesar, 86

Unfiltered Gin 22 (Dillon's Small Batch
    Distillers), 23
Ungava Premium Dry Gin (Domaine
    Pinnacle Microdistillerie), 23, 96
Urban Moonshine Organic Maple
    Digestive Bitters, 107
URSA, 106
UVA Wine & Cocktail, 56

Van Horne, Jeffrey, 135, 158
Vanilla-Infused Lot No. 40 Canadian
    Whisky, 107
Vecchio Amaro del Capo 1, 121
Veneto Tapa Lounge, 37, 54
verjus
    Celery-Verjus Shrub, 113
vermouth
    about, 9
    Acadian Driftwood, 142
    Arctic Martinez, 175
    Arctic Rose Vermouth Reduction,
        175
    Balsam Blend, 101
    Canadian Rye Dirty Martini, 118
    Classic Negroni, 150
    The Emperor, 56
    Fiddlehead Martini, 139
    The Gardiner, 108
    Gins & Needles, 77
    The Loose Jaw, 81
    Pear-Infused Vermouth, 56
    Winter Garden, 155
Victoria Spirits distillery, 23, 37, 56, 61,
    110, 184
vinho verde
    Sparkling Watermelon Sipper, 147
vintage rum, 9
violet liqueur
    Butchart Garden Swizzle, 61
vodka
    about, 10
    Blackberry Grenadine, 189
    The Boreal Cotton-Candy Cocktail,
        125
    Butchart Garden Swizzle, 61
    Canadian Rye Dirty Martini, 118
    Chinook Sangria, 71
    East–Meets–West Coast Caesar, 19
    Fiddlehead Martini, 139
    Flintabbatey Flonatin's Sunless City
        Sipper, 89
    The Great White Caesar, 18
    Labrador Iced Tea, 163
    The Pearl Punch, 73
    Raspberry Cordial, 190
    Rocket Richardonnay, 47
    Seamist Tea–Infused Vodka, 184
    Sour Slush, 28
    The Stampeder, 78
    Traditional-Style Grenadine, 189

Voisey, Kristen, 167

Walnut Orgeat, Black, 192
watermelon
    El Camino 2.0, 50
    Sparkling Watermelon Sipper, 147
    Watermelon and Campari–Infused
        Tequila, 50
West, 44, 46
What's Up, Doc? 54
wheat beer. See also beer
    Saskatoon Berry & Wheat Beer
        Cocktail, 84
whisky, 10. See also bourbon; Canadian
    whisky; Irish whiskey; Scotch;
    unaged whisky
Whisky-Soaked Wild Fruit, 101
white rum, 114
    The 52%, 166
    The Canadian R&R, 114
    Earl Grey–Infused Rum, 166
    Labrador Iced Tea, 163
    The Nellie J. Banks, 148
white wine
    Black Sesame Syrup, 102
    Chardonnay-Maple Reduction, 47
    Kir, 24
    Peary Punch, 110
    Prince Edward Bounty, 117
    Riesling Syrup, 111
Whoop-Up Bug Juice, 68
Wild Blueberry Shrub, 166
Wild Rose Liqueur (Rossignol Estate
    Winery), 150
Wild Rose Negroni, 150
wine. See dessert wine; port; Prosecco;
    red wine; sparkling wine; white
    wine
Winegarden Estate, 134
Winter Garden, 155
Wiser's (Canadian whisky), 178, 185
Wolowidnyk, David, 44
Woo, Matt, 195
Wray & Nephew, 148

Yukon Brewing, 170
Yukon Gold Rush, 173
Yukon Jack Liqueur
    Yukon Gold Rush, 173
    The Yukon Sourtoe Shot, 178
Yukon Shine Distillery, 23, 170, 175, 176
The Yukon Sourtoe Shot, 178
Yukon Spirits, 170

SCOTT MCCALLUM's cocktail obsession and alchemist-like knack for creating drinkable delights has led to a home bar that's bursting at the seams. It's loaded with an array of homemade bitters, colourful infused spirits and enough equipment to fill a small kitchen.

Scott has over a decade of service experience, which he's acquired in tandem with his acting career. He's managed a Montreal B&B, worked at Canada's iconic Massey Hall and spent some time slinging drinks at his favourite local.

This seriously patriotic Canuck has set foot in almost every province and territory in Canada. These travels have broadened his knowledge for all the potable potential this country has to offer. The impact of these experiences has inspired him to develop a collection of handcrafted cocktails that embrace Canada and its terroir.

VICTORIA WALSH's favourite place is the kitchen, where she creates, discovers and experiments with all things food and drink. Whether she's writing about great eats, inventing and testing new recipes, or unwinding with a glass of wine and a piece of cheese, Victoria gives her kitchen plenty of quality time—and her kitchen always gives back!

After Victoria received her certificate in chef training from the acclaimed program at George Brown College, she apprenticed as both a chef and pastry chef and honed her skills in kitchens across Toronto. Victoria earned her chops as a writer and recipe developer while working as associate food editor at *Chatelaine* and compiling, editing and developing the *Chatelaine Modern Classics* cookbook. She is a freelance writer, editor, recipe developer/tester and food stylist. Her work has been featured in *The Globe and Mail*, *Food & Drink*, *Flare*, *Glow*, *Toronto Life* and many more.